Recipes From Our Front Porch

Hemlock Inn
Bryson City, North Carolina

Compiled by Ella Jo and John Shell
Artwork by Dianne Shell Hylton
Photography by Ed Sharp of Cherokee

Cover...

Our guests return year after year. Here on our front porch, they meet new friends and renew old acquaintances through the years. At our early morning coffee, served on the patio, not only is the day started in a majestic setting; but, our guests share knowledge of our world out there and recipes and talk about our food served here—thus the title of our cookbook: RECIPES FROM OUR FRONT PORCH.

**Photo by Cline Advertising—Gatlinburg, Tennessee 37738
(Photo of Swain County Courthouse by Cline also.)**

First Printing - 10,000
Second Printing - 5,000

International Standard Book Number 0-939-11465-8

Printed in the USA by

WIMMER
The Wimmer Companies, Inc.
Memphis

This book is lovingly dedicated

to

Doris and A.R. Tyson

who believed we could

by their encouragement and assistance

and

Velda and W.H. Woody

who proved we could

by staying all Season for 17 years

Introduction

There's a bend in the road on Galbraith Creek where an old apple tree grows very near the curve. I remember the first time I saw it. A calmness came over me that I hadn't experienced before. It was early spring with snow on the surrounding mountain peaks, but tiny buds were already visible on the old tree. Since then, twenty-six springs have come and gone and everytime I get to that bend in the road, I still find peace and serenity — whether spring, summer, fall or winter!

That's the feeling at Hemlock Inn. It's a special place! It would be impossible to write a cookbook without telling a little about the place where all this good food is cooked and served so bountifully...

Est. 1952

Original Line Drawing by Elizabeth Atherton

4

History

Hemlock Inn opened July 4, 1952. In the late 1940's, Lorene and Seth Haynie bought a mountain farm from Plumer Plemmons. Lorene was in charge of food service at Emory University and Seth was a realtor in Decatur, Ga. Their idea was a small mountain inn, and the original building had only nine rooms; but before ten years had passed, twelve more rooms and four cottages had been added, and we had been honored by being featured in *Country Inns and Back Roads.*

At first the Inn was open during the summer only. Later the fall season and then the spring season were added. Hemlock Inn operated two years without a telephone. (We still just have telephones in the office area, no televisions nor swimming pool.) The middle Lazy Susan dining room table is the original one. The other four were made in local cabinet shops.

Georgia and Raymond Johnson bought the Inn in 1964. We bought it in 1969. All three owners came from Georgia: the Haynies from Decatur, the Johnsons from Washington and the Shells from Marietta. All owners have resided at the Inn year-round.

The Hemlock Inn is on a 65-acre tract atop a small mountain at an elevation of about 2300 feet. We're one mile off Hwy. 19. We're three miles from the Great Smoky Mountains National Park, Deep Creek area.

Our basic philosophy has not changed in these past thirty years. Our goal is to give our guests a change: a refreshing place to get away for plenty of rest, relaxation...and...good food...

Acknowledgments

...would not be complete without thanks to Lorene Haynie who set up the recipes and many of the menus that are still used after forty-four years of trial. Also to the memory of two wonderful cooks and good friends: Annie Sitton, the first cook; and Myrtle Mask who stayed with us for twenty years and sixteen years respectively. They gave so much of themselves to the Inn. It would be impossible to mention all the fantastic help through the years - faithful and loyal - they've made Hemlock Inn what it is! We're always so afraid of leaving out someone who should be mentioned so we'll just say to those of you (both past and present) who have made the Inn the special place it is — thanks! Without an excellent staff, no place survives. All have been local people: house-wives, high school and college students.

Special thanks to Sally Jenkins and Doris Tyson who took time out from busy daily activities to proofread this book.

To all of you who buy this cookbook and will read a recipe you've given us during the years—thanks! Some have been named for you, others we just inherited.

We've also included some favorites of the Shell/Stevens families that have been tried and tested through the years that we don't usually serve at the Inn.

We could not possibly write a cookbook without giving thanks to our daughters, Dianne Shell Hylton and Elaine Shell White. Dianne did the drawings throughout the cookbook for us. "Lainey" has always given me such confidence in believing that I could cook for her many friends when she called to say she was bringing home twenty instead of six. I'm sure there were times the food wasn't as good as she led me to believe...And to John Lewis Shell who has lived with this cooking for forty-five years and still loves me...Thanks!

Basic Information

There will be two obvious deletions for those of you who are frequent guests at Hemlock: apple and pumpkin chips. These are preserves that are kept especially for serving each night at dinner and to sell in our Inn only. We think Mrs. Haynie's idea not to publish the recipe a good one. You will have to come to Hemlock Inn to enjoy our chips with a delicious meal served on our Lazy Susan tables. This will give you a sample of the food in this cookbook. At mealtimes, John always says the Blessing... some of which we have included here.

There are no short cuts to excellent meals. There are four cooks in our kitchen from before seven in the morning until after seven in the evening (working two shifts). We make our own bread crumbs from left-over rolls and biscuits. All our frying is done in peanut oil. We are aware of too much salt and sugar in our diets so we try to be careful with our preparation. We cook with gas at the Hemlock Inn. You must remember that all ovens are different and since your altitude may be different from ours (2300 feet), you will need to adjust your oven temperature and length of baking time according to your situation. All good cooks "fool around" with recipes and come up with good results. Feel free to do this with ours—good luck!

No cookbook could be a complete edition. I'm sure there will be many mistakes on my part and things left out that should've been included. So forgive this inexperienced writer who only under pressure from the marvelous guests of the Hemlock Inn insisted that I could do it—I undertake this not to prove myself an expert; but to share a special part of our living with you: *Food for body and soul* - Ella Jo's recipes and John's blessings...

Ella Jo Shell, Hemlock Inn

Our dear
   Heavenly Father,
how glad we are
   to start this day with Thee,
and we pray
that somehow Thou would help us to see
that it is not what comes our way
   that counts,
but rather what we do
with what comes our way.
We thank Thee
for Thy strength and mercy and now for this food.
                         In Jesus' name we ask it. Amen.

CONTENTS

Our
    dear Heavenly Father,
we are blessed
because we know Thee, and we
come now to give Thee Thanks.
    We are so glad
Thou dost love us, and call us
    by our first name and our prayer
is that we would do what is pleasing to Thee.
We thank Thee for this lovely day and for Thy love,
and for watching over our families. We thank Thee for this food now.
                            In Jesus' name we ask it. Amen.

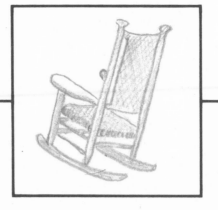

Beverages

HOT CHOCOLATE MIX

1 1-pound 9-ounce box powdered milk
1 6-ounce jar powdered coffee cream
1 large box powdered chocolate mix
1 1-pound box powdered sugar

Mix all together well. Store in an air-tight container. Use 3 heaping teaspoons in a cup of boiling water. Yield: Approximately 1 gallon or 80 servings.

AGNES' MOCHA PUNCH

1 2-ounce jar instant coffee
4 cups water
3 cups sugar
6 cups vanilla ice cream
6 cups chocolate ice cream
2 cups chocolate syrup
1 gallon milk

Mix instant coffee, water and sugar together and bring to boil (do not boil). Let simmer for 5 minutes. Combine milk and syrup. Add ice cream. Stir well. Yield: Serves 25.

12

TIM'S RUSSIAN TEA

1 gallon water
2 cups sugar
1 tablespoon cinnamon
2 teaspoons cloves
4 tea bags
1 pint water
1 14-fluid ounce can
  unsweetened pineapple juice

1 14-fluid ounce can
  unsweetened orange juice
1½ cups fresh or frozen orange
  juice
¾ cup fresh or frozen lemon
  juice

Boil 1 gallon water, sugar, cinnamon and cloves together for 5 minutes. Let 4 tea bags steep in 1 pint of water for 5 minutes. Add mixtures together and add juices. Let mixture simmer for about 30 minutes. Serve hot. Yield: 1½ gallons.

LIB'S ALMOND PUNCH

6 cups pineapple juice	1 tablespoon almond flavoring
1 quart ginger ale	½ cup sugar

Add all ingredients together. May add more sugar and flavoring if desired. Yield: Serves 12.

ANNIE'S INSTANT SPICED TEA

1 1-pound 2-ounce jar powdered orange drink mix	1½-2 cups sugar
¾ cup instant tea	1 teaspoon ground cloves
1 3-ounce package powdered lemonade mix	1 teaspoon ground cinnamon

Mix all ingredients well. (Spices can be increased if desired.) Use 2 well-rounded teaspoons to cup of boiling water for each serving of tea. Yield: Approximately 1 quart.

NANCY'S TEA PUNCH

4 cups water
6 tea bags
½ cup sugar
1 8-ounce can frozen lemonade

1 lemonade can of water
1 12-ounce can pineapple juice
1 8-ounce ginger ale or lemon-
  lime carbonated drink

Brew tea for several hours. *Very strong!* Add other ingredients. Yield: Serves 12.

MILLIE'S HOT MILLED CIDER

1 gallon apple cider
1 gallon cranberry juice
12 whole cloves

2 cinnamon sticks
dash of allspice
1 cup sugar

Combine all ingredients in saucepan and heat until sugar is dissolved. Cool and reheat. (Best if prepared the day before it is to be served.) Yield: Serves 25.

Our
   Heavenly Father,
we would truly
come unto Thee this new day.
   We come
because of our need
   and not because of our worth.
We pray that somehow we might learn
to walk with Thee in a way that is pleasing to Thee.
We thank thee for Thy strength, and now for this food.
                     In Jesus' name we ask it. Amen.

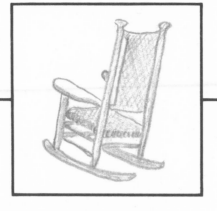

Breads

HEMLOCK INN YEAST ROLLS

¾ cup scalded milk
⅛ cup sugar
3 tablespoons oil
1 teaspoon salt

1 tablespoon yeast
¼ cup lukewarm water
1 slightly beaten egg
3½ cups flour

Put milk on to warm. Put yeast and lukewarm water in bowl. Make rounded spoonfuls - be generous. Put sugar and oil in mixing bowl. Beat egg in small bowl. Mix milk, yeast and egg with sugar and oil. Mix *well!* Put in a small amount of flour and add salt. Beat until air bubbles appear. Gradually add more flour until stiff. Cover with melted butter and let rise until double. *Don't let set after dough rises!* Roll and cut; fold over. Butter and let rise again. We use melted margarine. Bake at 500º-550º for about 10 minutes. Yield: 6 dozen rolls.

To make whole wheat rolls, use ⅓ whole wheat to ⅔ white flour.

HEMLOCK INN BISCUITS

6 cups self-rising flour
3 tablespoons baking powder

½ cup pure lard
1 cup buttermilk

Mix all ingredients together. Mix together with hands until very thick consistency. Split dough in half. Roll each half in flour with rolling pin to ¼-inch to ⅜-inch thickness. Use biscuit cutter dipped in flour to cut biscuits. Place on baking sheet used only for baking biscuits or rolls. Paint tops with buttermilk. Bake at 500º on bottom of oven for 5 minutes. Raise to next rack and bake until golden brown - approximately 8-10 minutes more. Yield: 8 dozen small biscuits.

COOK'S REFRIGERATED ROLLS

4 tablespoons yeast	¾ cup shortening
1 cup warm water	¾ cup sugar
4 well-beaten eggs	4 teaspoons salt
4 cups hot water	16 cups flour

Mix yeast in warm water. Beat eggs. Set aside. Mix together hot water, shortening, sugar and salt. Let cool to luke warm. Add yeast and eggs. Stir in about 16 cups flour or enough to make a soft dough. Store in refrigerator. Pinch out and let rise. Bake in preheated oven of 500° for about 10 minutes. Yield: 6 dozen.

CORN BREAD

2 cups self-rising cornmeal	¼ cup melted bacon grease
¼ cup self-rising flour	2 cups buttermilk
1 egg	

Beat egg slightly. Add other ingredients. Pour into well-greased, hot black skillet. Bake in 450° oven for 25-30 minutes. Yield: Serves 10.

CORN MUFFINS

2 cups self-rising cornmeal	1 teaspoon sugar
¼ cup self-rising flour	¼ cup melted bacon grease
2 eggs	1 cup milk

Beat egg slightly. Add other ingredients. Pour into greased muffin pans and bake in 400° oven for 15-20 minutes. Yield: 18.

PALACE SPOON BREAD

2 cups meal
1 quart boiling water
1 teaspoon salt

¼ cup butter
3 beaten eggs
2 cups milk

Sprinkle meal into boiling water. Stir for 1 minute. Remove from heat. Add eggs and beat well. Add milk and whip. Pour into a well-greased, 1½-quart baking dish. Bake in 350⁰ oven for 40-50 minutes. Test for doneness in center of bread. Serve immediately. Yield: Serves 6.

RUTH KELLEY'S EGG BREAD

1½ cups scalded milk
1½ cups white corn meal
1 teaspoon salt

2 tablespoons melted shortening
2½ teaspoons baking powder
1 beaten egg

Mix all ingredients together. Bake in 400⁰ oven for 20 minutes. Yield: Serves 8.

EMILY'S JALEPENO CORNBREAD

2 beaten eggs
½ cup vegetable oil
1 small can cream-style corn
2 medium chopped onions
½ chopped bell pepper

2 cups self-rising corn meal
1 cup buttermilk
1 chopped jalepeno pepper
½ cup grated sharp cheddar
   cheese

Grease oblong baking dish. Sprinkle with corn meal. Mix eggs, oil, corn, onion, bell pepper, corn meal, buttermilk and jalepeno pepper together. Pour half of batter in pan. Sprinkle half of grated cheese over batter. Pour remaining batter over cheese, then add remaining cheese. Bake at 400⁰-450⁰ oven until brown. Yield: Serves 8.

MOTHER'S BRAN BREAD

1 cup bran	1 envelope yeast
½ cup sugar	1 cup lukewarm water
2 teaspoons salt	2 eggs
1 cup shortening	6 cups flour
1 cup boiling water	

Mix bran, sugar, salt, shortening and boiling water together. Set aside and cool. In separate bowl, dissolve yeast in lukewarm water; and add to bran mixture. Slowly add 2 eggs (room temperature) and flour. Let rise until double. Punch down. Divide and place in well greased bread pans which have been floured. *Do not preheat oven.* Bake at 325⁰ oven for 40 minutes. Yield: 4 loaves.

PROTEIN BREAD

4 cups warm water	2 teaspoons cider vinegar
4 tablespoons yeast	3 cups gluten flour
2 teaspoons salt	1 cup soy flour
4 teaspoons sugar	5 cups whole wheat flour

Dissolve yeast in water. Add sugar, salt and vinegar. Slowly add soy and gluten flour; then add whole wheat flour. Mix slowly until dough stiffens and does not stick. Knead well for about 5 minutes. Put in your favorite bread-baking pans. Let rise in warm place. Bake in 325⁰ oven for about 1 hour or until brown. Yield: 4 loaves.

MIL'S PINEAPPLE MUFFINS

4 cups self-rising flour
3 teaspoons soda
4 cups corn meal
8 tablespoons brown sugar
8 eggs

6 cups buttermilk
2 cups drained crushed
  pineapple
1 cup bacon grease

Sift flour, soda, corn meal and sugar together. Slightly beat eggs and add buttermilk, pineapple and bacon grease to flour mixture. Grease muffin pans well and fill ⅔ full of mixture. Top with bacon bits. Bake in 425° oven for 15 to 20 minutes. Yield: 4 dozen.

SWEET POTATO MUFFINS

2 cups cooked mashed sweet
  potatoes
2¼ cups flour
1½ cups milk
3 eggs
2¼ cups whole wheat flour
¾ cup melted butter or
  margarine

1 cup sugar
6 teaspoons baking powder
1½ teaspoons cinnamon
1½ teaspoons nutmeg
1½ teaspoons cloves
1½ cups raisins

Sift together flour, baking powder, cinnamon, nutmeg, cloves and sugar. Mix together sweet potatoes, milk, eggs, margarine and raisins. Add to dry ingredients. Put in well greased muffin pans. Bake in 400° oven for 20 minutes. Yield: 4 dozen.

MIL'S APPLESAUCE MUFFINS

2 cups applesauce
2 sticks melted margarine
2 cups sugar
2 eggs
1 teaspoon vanilla
4 cups flour

1 teaspoon cloves
3 teaspoons cinnamon
2 teaspoons allspice
2 teaspoons soda
1 cup chopped nuts

Sift together all dry ingredients. Mix eggs, applesauce, vanilla and nuts together, and add to dry ingredients. Bake in greased muffin pans in 425° oven for 15 to 20 minutes. Keep well refrigerated and use as needed. Yield: 4 dozen.

GINGER MUFFINS

1¼ cups shortening
1 cup sugar
4 eggs
1 cup dark syrup
4 cups flour

2 teaspoons powdered ginger
2 teaspoons soda
½ teaspoon salt
½ teaspoon cinnamon
1 cup buttermilk

Cream shortening and sugar. Add eggs, one at a time. Mix dry ingredients and add; alternating with buttermilk and syrup to the first mixture. Mix well and cover bowl before placing in refrigerator. Cook in greased tins. Bake in 400° oven for 10 to 12 minutes. The uncooked mixture will keep indefinitely in refrigerator, if you will just spoon out mixture as needed. *Do not stir again.* Yield: 4 dozen.

23

Our Heavenly Father,
  again how happy we are
to truly come to Thee,
and we come
  because of our needs,
and not
because of our pride.
We thank you for this lovely day,
and Thy continued mercy.
We know that you love us because you suffer with us.
Thank you now for these friends, and this food.
                    In Jesus' name we ask it. Amen.

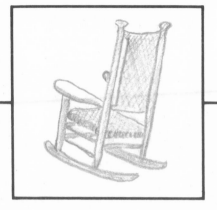

Cakes & Frostings

MOTHER'S CHOCOLATE CAKE

2 cups flour
2 cups sugar
1 cup water
1 cup oil
1 stick butter

4 tablespoons cocoa
½ cup buttermilk
2 eggs
½ teaspoon soda
pinch of salt

Combine flour and sugar in mixing bowl. Put water, oil, butter and cocoa into heavy boiler. Bring to a boil and cook one minute, stirring constantly. Add mixture to sugar and flour and beat well. Add buttermilk, eggs, soda and salt. Pour batter in 13x9x3-inch pan and bake in 350° oven for 40 minutes. Ice while still hot. Yield: Serves 18.

ICING FOR CHOCOLATE CAKE

4 tablespoons milk
4 tablespoons cocoa
1 stick butter

1 teaspoon vanilla
2 cups powdered sugar

Mix milk, cocoa, butter together and bring to boil. Add powdered sugar, stirring until well mixed. Ice in pan while still hot. Yield: Icing for 1 cake.

GERMAN CHOCOLATE POUND CAKE

1 4-ounce bar sweet German
  chocolate
2 cups sugar
1 cup shortening
4 eggs
2 teaspoons vanilla

2 teaspoons butter flavoring
1 cup buttermilk
3 cups sifted flour
½ teaspoon soda
1 teaspoon salt

Partially melt chocolate over hot water. Remove and stir rapidly until melted. Cool. Cream sugar and shortening. Add well-beaten eggs, flavoring and buttermilk. Sift together flour, soda and salt. Add to shortening and mix well. Blend in chocolate. Pour into well-greased and floured 9-inch tube pan. Bake in 300° oven for about 1½ hours. Remove from pan while still hot and place under tightly fitted cover until thoroughly cooled. Yield: 1 cake.

SWEET CHOCOLATE CAKE GLAZE

1 4-ounce bar sweet German
  chocolate
1 tablespoon butter
¼ cup water

1 cup sifted powdered sugar
dash of salt
½ teaspoon vanilla

Melt chocolate and butter in water over low heat. Mix in sugar and salt. Blend together and add vanilla. For thinner glaze, add a small amount of hot water. Yield: ¾ cup.

27

CHOCOLATE POUND CAKE

2 sticks margarine
½ cup shortening
3 cups sugar
5 eggs
3 cups flour

¼ teaspoon salt
½ teaspoon baking powder
½ cup cocoa
1¼ cups milk
1 teaspoon vanilla

Cream margarine, shortening and sugar together well. Add eggs one at a time, blending well after each. Sift together flour, salt, baking powder and cocoa. Add alternately with milk. Add vanilla. Pour into greased and floured tube pan and bake in 325⁰ oven for 1 hour and 25 minutes. Yield: 1 cake.

HEMLOCK INN BIRTHDAY CAKE

1 cup shortening
2 cups sugar
3 cups flour
¾ teaspoon salt

1 teaspoon baking powder
1 cup milk
1 teaspoon vanilla flavoring
4 eggs

Cream shortening and add sugar. Add eggs one at a time. Sift flour, salt and baking powder. Add alternately flour mixture with milk. Fill greased 1-pound coffee can half full. Bake in 350⁰ oven for 1 hour. Yield: 4 small cakes.

SPICE CAKE

1 cup quick oatmeal	1⅓ cups flour
1¼ cups boiling water	1 teaspoon soda
½ cup shortening	½ teaspoon salt
1 cup brown sugar	½ teaspoon cinnamon
1 cup sugar	½ teaspoon nutmeg
2 eggs	1 teaspoon vanilla

Pour boiling water over oatmeal. Let stand 10 minutes. Cream shortening, brown sugar and white sugar. Add to oatmeal mixture. Add eggs one at a time. Sift flour, soda, salt, cinnamon, nutmeg and add to mixture. Stir just enough to mix. Add vanilla. Pour into greased 9x13-inch pan and bake in 325⁰ oven for 35-40 minutes. Yield: Serves 18.

TOPPING FOR SPICE CAKE

1 stick margarine	1 cup well-drained crushed
1 cup brown sugar	pineapple
2 egg yolks	1 cup nuts

Cream margarine, sugar and egg yolks together. Add pineapple and nuts (if desired - we use one or the other). Spread on cooked cake. Brown under broiler. Serve warm. Yield: Icing 1 cake.

PAT'S CARROT CAKE

1½ cups flour	⅔ cup peanut oil
1 cup sugar	2 eggs
1 teaspoon baking powder	1 cup finely shredded carrots
1 teaspoon soda	½ cup crushed pineapple
1 teaspoon cinnamon	with syrup
½ teaspoon salt	1 teaspoon vanilla

Mix all dry ingredients together. Add oil, eggs, carrots, crushed pine-apple, and vanilla. Beat 2 minutes at medium speed on electric mixer. Bake in greased and lightly floured 9x9x2-inch pan in 350° oven about 35 minutes. Yield: Serves 12.

ICING FOR CARROT CAKE

1 3-ounce package softened cream cheese	1 teaspoon vanilla
1 tablespoon softened butter	2 cups powdered sugar

Beat all ingredients together until light and fluffy. If necessary, add milk to make spreading easy. Yield: Frosting for 1 cake.

RAW APPLE CAKE

2 cups sugar	1 teaspoon mace
1 cup margarine	2 teaspoons soda
4 beaten eggs	1 cup cold coffee
½ teaspoon salt	3 cups raw chopped apples
3 cups flour	1 cup raisins
2 teaspoons cinnamon	1 cup nuts

Cream sugar and margarine. Add eggs. Sift salt, flour, cinnamon, mace and soda. Add alternately with coffee. Add apples, raisins and nuts. Bake in 350° oven for 1 hour or until firm. Sprinkle with powdered sugar. Yield: 1 tube pan cake.

DOT'S PRUNE CAKE

3 eggs	1 teaspoon nutmeg
1 cup oil	1 teaspoon allspice
2 cups flour	1 cup buttermilk
1 cup cooked and cut prunes	1 cup chopped nuts
1½ cup sugar	1 teaspoon vanilla
1 teaspoon soda	½ teaspoon salt
1 teaspoon cinnamon	

Mix sugar and oil together. Add eggs. Sift together flour, soda, cinnamon, nutmeg, allspice and add alternately with buttermilk. Add prunes, nuts and vanilla. Pour into buttered tube pan or standard sheet cake pan. Bake in 350° oven for 45 minutes (or until brown). Remove from oven and add icing while cake is still hot. Yield: Serves 18.

ICING FOR PRUNE CAKE

1 cup sugar	1 teaspoon white corn syrup
½ cup buttermilk	¼ cup butter
½ teaspoon soda	½ teaspoon vanilla

Mix all ingredients together in heavy saucepan and boil until drop in cold water forms ball. Pour over cake while still hot. It will soak into cake. Yield: Icing for 1 cake.

SWEET POTATO SURPRISE CAKE

1½ cups peanut oil
2 cups sugar
4 eggs
3 tablespoons hot water
2½ cups sifted flour
3 teaspoons baking powder

¼ teaspoon salt
1 teaspoon ground cinnamon
1 teaspoon nutmeg
1½ cups grated sweet potatoes
1 cup chopped nuts
1 teaspoon vanilla

Combine oil, sugar and beat well until smooth. Add egg yolks and beat. Add hot water and dry ingredients which have been sifted together. Stir in sweet potatoes, nuts and vanilla. Beat well. Beat egg whites until stiff and fold into mixture. Bake in greased 9x13-inch pan in 350° oven for 25-30 minutes. Cool and frost. Yield: Serves 12.

FROSTING FOR SWEET POTATO CAKE

1 14½-ounce can evaporated
   milk
1 cup sugar
½ cup margarine

3 egg yolks
1 teaspoon vanilla
1⅓ cups flaked coconut

Combine milk, sugar, margarine, egg yolks and vanilla in heavy boiler and cook about 12 minutes until thick, stirring constantly. Remove from heat and add coconut. Beat until cool and frost cake. Yield: 1 cake.

MISS BETTY'S CHERRY CAKE COBBLER

1 stick margarine
1¾ cups sugar
1 cup flour
2 teaspoons baking powder

¾ cup milk
1 16-ounce can pie cherries
   and juice
½ teaspoon almond flavoring

Melt margarine in cobbler pan. Mix ¾ cup sugar, flour, baking powder and milk together. Pour into melted margarine. Stir a little. Mix 1 cup sugar with cherries and juice and bring to boil. Pour over batter mixture. Distribute cherries evenly with spoon. Bake in 350° oven for about 45 minutes. Yield: Serves 8.

E. J.'S CHRISTMAS CAKE

1 angel food cake
1 quart peppermint ice cream

1 pint whipping cream
½ cup crushed peppermint stick

Slice angel cake into 3 layers. Put bottom layer on your favorite cake plate. Put about 2 inches of peppermint ice cream on top of cake, cover with 2nd layer. Put another 2 inches on ice cream, and put on top layer of cake. Whip cream. Ice cake with whipping cream. (May use dream whip if you're dieting!) Sprinkle crushed peppermint stick over top. Freeze. Cut and serve as desired. Yield: Serves 16.

MYRTLE'S BUTTERNUT POUND CAKE

3 cups sugar
½ pound butter
½ cup shortening
5 eggs
3 cups measured and sifted flour

½ teaspoon baking powder
¼ teaspoon salt
1 tablespoon butternut
   flavoring
1 cup milk

Blend shortening, butter, and sugar until creamy. Add eggs one at a time, beating after each. Sift dry ingredients together and add alternately with milk. Pour in greased tube pan and bake in 350° oven for 1 hour and 15 minutes. Yield: 1 cake.

Our
   dear Heavenly Father,
Thou dost put a song
   in our heart and we pause now
to sing Thy praise.
We come
simply to lift our hands and hearts
   to Thee in worship,
and give thanks for this lovely day and for Thy mercy.
We are so thankful that Thou dost continue to struggle with us.
Thank you now for these friends and for this food.
                         In Jesus' name we ask it. Amen.

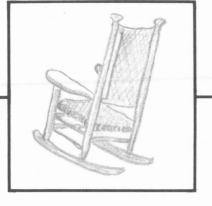

Candies & Cookies

ICE BOX COOKIES

1 cup brown sugar
1 cup white sugar
¾ cup melted margarine or
    butter

¾ cup melted shortening
1 teaspoon vanilla
2 slightly beaten eggs
4 cups flour

Mix sugar with melted margarine and shortening. Add eggs. Sift in flour and add vanilla. Mold in about 12 inch rolls, wrap in waxed paper and put in refrigerator or freezer. Bake in 350° oven for 10 to 12 minutes. Yield: 5 dozen.

Used in Hemlock Inn box lunches.

REFRIGERATOR COOKIES

1 cup margarine
1 cup sugar
1 cup brown sugar
2 eggs
1 teaspoon soda

1 teaspoon salt
3½ cups flour
½ tablespoon brandy or rum
½ tablespoon butter flavoring
1 cup black walnuts

Cream margarine, white and brown sugar together. Fold in eggs. Add flavoring and brandy or rum. Sift soda, salt and flour and stir enough flour into above for soft dough. Add balance flour by hand. Roll into long rolls 2 inches in diameter. Wrap, refrigerate and slice later and bake at 350° oven for 10 to 12 minutes. Yield: 4 dozen cookies.

FAVORITE OATMEAL COOKIES

1 cup shortening	½ teaspoon baking powder
1 cup sugar	½ teaspoon salt
1 cup brown sugar	2 cups quick cooking oatmeal
2 eggs	1 cup seedless raisins
2 cups sifted flour	½ cup chopped nuts
1 teaspoon soda	

Cream shortening and sugar. Add eggs and beat well. Sift together flour, baking powder, soda, and salt. Add to creamed mixture. Stir well. Stir in oatmeal, raisins and nuts. Drop dough from a teaspoon 2 inches apart on a greased cookie sheet. Bake at 350⁰ for 10 to 12 minutes or until light brown. Allow to cool a minute before removing from cookie sheet. Yield: 6 dozen.

BUTTERSCOTCH OATMEAL COOKIES

1 cup margarine	2 cups flour
2 cups brown sugar	1 teaspoon baking powder
2 eggs	½ teaspoon soda
2 teaspoons vanilla	1 teaspoon salt
1 teaspoon butter flavoring	1 cup pecans
4 cups rolled oates	

Melt margarine, beat in sugar. Add eggs, vanilla and butter flavoring. Beat well. Mix oats, flour, baking powder, soda and salt. Add to mixture. Stir in pecans. Drop on cookie sheet in ½ teaspoon size. Bake in 350⁰ oven for 12 minutes. Yield: 5 dozen.

BETTY CASS' BROWN SUGAR COOKIES

2 cups brown sugar
½ cup shortening
½ cup margarine
2 eggs

2¼ cups self-rising flour
2 teaspoons vanilla
1 cup chopped nuts

Cream shortening, add sugar and eggs. Sift in flour and add vanilla and nuts. Drop by teaspoons on buttered pan. Bake at 350° for 15 minutes. Yield: 3 dozen.

CATHEDRAL COOKIES

1 12-ounce package chocolate
   chips
4 tablespoons butter
2 eggs
½ teaspoon vanilla

¼ teaspoon salt
1 10½-ounce package miniature
   colored marshmallows
1 cup chopped pecans

Melt chocolate chips in top of double boiler over hot water. Add butter and mix well. Beat eggs well for 2 minutes and add to chocolate mixture. Add vanilla and salt. Cook for 2 minutes. Take top pan off and let cool. Add marshmallows and nuts. Cover waxed paper with powdered sugar. Divide batter into thirds. Roll into long rolls 2-inches in diameter. Chill overnight. Slice off when needed. Keep indefinitely in refrigerator. Freezes well. Yield: 3 dozen.

MOLASSES COOKIES

1 cup brown sugar
1 egg
1 cup molasses
¾ cup melted butter

¼ cup boiling water
salt to taste
flour

Slightly beat egg, add sugar, molasses, butter, water and salt. Add just enough flour to knead. Roll, cut out with your favorite cookie cutter and bake in 400° oven for 8-10 minutes. Yield: 24.

MELANIE'S COOKIES

1 cup shortening
1 teaspoon salt
1 teaspoon grated lemon rind
1 teaspoon nutmeg
2 cups sugar

4 eggs
2 teaspoons baking powder
4 cups flour
1 teaspoon soda
¼ cup milk

Beat together the shortening, salt, lemon rind, nutmeg, sugar, and eggs until smooth. Add baking powder and soda to flour and add milk. Add to egg mixture. Drop by teaspoon on greased cookie sheet. Flatten with bottom of glass, covered with damp cloth. Sprinkle with sugar and bake in 300° oven for 15-18 minutes. Yield: 5 dozen.

CHOCOLATE STARLITE MINT SURPRISES

3 cups flour
1 teaspoon soda
½ teaspoon salt
½ cup butter
½ cup shortening
1 box solid chocolate candy
   wafers

½ cup brown sugar
1 cup granulated sugar
2 eggs
2 tablespoons water
1 teaspoon vanilla
24 pecan halves

Sift flour, soda and salt together. Cream butter and sugar well. Blend in eggs, unbeaten. Beat well and add dry ingredients gradually with water and vanilla. Refrigerate for at least 2 hours. Mold dough ½ teaspoon at a time around wafer. *Sometimes hard to find - usually available in chain grocery store candy counter.* If desired, place pecan on top. Bake in 375° oven for 10 to 12 minutes. Yield: 2 dozen.

NANCY'S CRUNCHY DATE BARS

1 stick butter
1 cup brown sugar
1 8-ounce package dates
2 cups rice krispies

½ cup coconut
1 teaspoon vanilla
½ cup pecans

Cook butter, sugar over medium heat 10 to 15 minutes; stirring well. Cut dates in halves and cook with butter and sugar. Mash dates and let mixture cool. Add coconut, vanilla, nuts and rice krispies. After shaping in little cigar shapes, roll in powdered sugar. Yield: 3 dozen.

ELLEN'S NO-FLOUR COOKIE

1 egg   1 cup crunchy peanut butter
1 cup brown sugar

Slightly beat egg and add brown sugar. Mix in peanut butter. Drop onto cookie sheet in ½ teaspoonfuls. Bake in 350° oven for 10-12 minutes. Yield: 24.

PEANUT BUTTER STICKS

Trim stale bread, cut into sticks. Dry completely. Toast lightly. Mix ½ cup of peanut oil and ½ cup of peanut butter together. Dip dry sticks into mix. Roll in fine crumbs made from crust. Let dry. Yield: 24.

BOOTSIE'S HEAVENLY HASH

5 4-ounce bars milk chocolate
1 package 6¼-ounces miniature
   marshmallows

1 cup broken black walnuts

Melt chocolate over boiling water. Stir until smooth. Blend in marshmallows and nuts until coated with chocolate. Pour into greased 9x13-inch pan and refrigerate until firm. Yield: 36.

AUNT POLLY'S DIVINITY

2 cups sugar
½ cup water
½ cup light corn syrup

2 stiffly beaten egg whites
1 teaspoon vanilla
1 cup chopped pecans

Cook to soft ball stage the sugar, water and corn syrup. Pour *half* of mixture into bowl with egg whites. Cook other half to hard ball stage. Fold in egg white mixture and add vanilla. Beat until stiff, add nuts and put on waxed paper in ¾ teaspoon balls to cool. Nut halves may be placed on top instead of chopped nuts in candy if desired. If it does not harden (heaven forbid!), cook over water for 10 or 15 minutes longer. Yield: 24 pieces.

GAMMY'S CREAMY PRALINES

1 cup firmly packed dark
  brown sugar
1 cup granulated sugar

⅔ cup undiluted evaporated milk
½ teaspoon vanilla
1 cup coarsely chopped pecans

Thoroughly combine brown sugar, granulated sugar and milk. Stirring constantly, cook over medium heat until mixture forms soft ball. Remove from heat, add vanilla and nuts. Beat until thick. Drop onto wax paper in small amounts. Yield: 18.

MOTHER'S CHOCOLATE FUDGE

3 cups sugar
½ cup evaporated milk
½ cup water
3 tablespoons corn syrup
⅓ cup cocoa

3 tablespoons butter
1 teaspoon vanilla
½-1 cup chopped nuts
¼ teaspoon salt

Mix sugar, cocoa, salt, and syrup with milk and water. Place in heavy sauce pan over medium heat and bring to boil. Stir often to keep from sticking. Cook rapidly until mixture forms a soft ball when dropped into a cup of cold water or until registers soft ball stage on candy thermometer. Start testing after cooking for 5 minutes. Remove from heat and add butter and vanilla. Let cool slightly and beat until spreading consistency. Add nuts and stir. Pour into a well buttered dish. Cool and cut into squares. Yield: 24 small pieces.

Our
Heavenly
  Father,
we continue
to be excited about
  Thy gospel,
and our prayer
  is this day we may
learn to express it better.
Our hearts are open wide that we might receive Thy grace,
and truly walk with Thee.
We thank Thee for a new opportunity, and for Thy strength, and
especially for this food.   In Jesus' name we ask it. Amen.

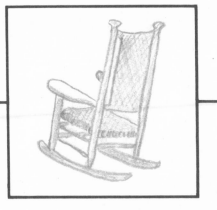

Desserts

CHOCOLATE TORTE

1 stick butter
1 cup flour
¾ cup chopped pecans
1 8-ounce package cream
  cheese
1 cup powdered sugar

1 9-ounce carton prepared
  whipped topping
1 family size package instant
  chocolate pudding
1 teaspoon almond flavoring

Melt butter in 9x13 baking dish. Sprinkle in flour and nuts and spread until smooth with spoon. Bake in 350° oven for 15 minutes. Let cool. Cream the cheese and sugar. Mix together 1 cup dream whip and cheese mixture. Spread over crust as first layer. Prepare instant chocolate pudding as directed and add flavoring. Spread over first layer. Top with remaining dream whip. Yield: Serves 12.

ANNETTE'S GLORIFIED BROWNIES

½ cup butter
1 cup sugar
2 eggs
1 teaspoon vanilla
1 dozen marshmallows

2 1-ounce squares chocolate
1 cup flour
1 tablespoon baking powder
1 cup chopped pecans

Cream butter and sugar. Add eggs that have been beaten well and vanilla. Add melted chocolate. Sift flour and baking powder together. Mix well and add to chocolate mixture. Add nuts. Pour into a greased 8 by 8 inch pan and bake at 350º for 30 minutes. When done, place marshmallows over top and return to oven until marshmallows are ready to spread. Remove from oven and cool. When cool, ice with chocolate icing:

1 tablespoon butter
¼ pound powdered sugar

½ cup cocoa

Cream butter and add sugar with cocoa. If mixture gets too thick, add a small amount of milk. Yield: 12.

BOOTSIE'S CHOCOLATE DREAM SQUARES

20 graham crackers
2 sticks butter
2 cups powdered sugar
3 eggs

3 squares 1-ounce chocolate
1½ cups chopped nuts
1 teaspoon vanilla

Roll out graham crackers to make crumbs. Melt butter and chocolate together and add to crumb mixture. Beat eggs and fold in sugar. Add vanilla and nuts. Put in greased 9x13-inch pan. Refrigerate overnight. Serve with whipping cream. Yield: Serves 12.

CHOCOLATE FUDGE SAUCE

½ pound chocolate
2 cups sugar
1 tablespoon butter

1 13-ounce can evaporated milk
pinch of salt
1 teaspoon vanilla

Melt chocolate and sugar over hot water. Add butter, milk, and salt. Stir well. Add vanilla. This can be used for cake icing. We thin with a small amount of warm water and use over ice cream. Keep in refrigerator for 2 weeks. Yield: Serves 20 sundaes.

CHOCOLATE LUSH

1 large angel food cake
1 12-ounce package chocolate
   chips
4 eggs
pinch of salt

½ cup milk
2 tablespoons sugar
1 pint whipping cream
1 teaspoon vanilla

Break cake into pieces and put half of cake into buttered 9x13-inch pan. Melt chocolate chips in top of double boiler. Remove from stove and add egg yolks. Add milk slowly. Add sugar to stiff beaten egg whites. Fold into egg yolks, chocolate and milk. Fold into whipped cream and vanilla. Pour half of mixture over cake. Add rest of cake and put remaining chocolate mixture on top. Chill overnight. Yield: Serves 12.

CHOCOLATE ECLAIR SQUARES

1½ boxes graham crackers
2 boxes instant French vanilla
  pudding

½ cup dream whip
1 8-ounce package frozen
  prepared whipped topping

Layer graham crackers in 9x13 pan. Mix pudding as directed on package. Fold in cool whip. Put 2nd layer of graham crackers and frost with prepared whipped topping.

FROSTING FOR ECLAIRS

1 stick butter
3 tablespoons cocoa

2 cups powdered sugar
1 egg

Melt butter and chocolate until dissolved. Remove from heat. Add sugar. Beat until slightly cooled and add egg. Pour over cake. Refrigerate. Yield: Serves 18.

FROZEN APRICOT DELIGHT

6 egg yolks
pinch salt
1 cup sugar
4 tablespoons apricot jam
1 cup apricots pureed

2 cups whipping cream or
  prepared whipped topping
2 cups vanilla wafer crumbs
4 tablespoons lemon juice
6 egg whites

Beat egg yolks, salt and 1 cup sugar. Add pureed apricots, jam and lemon juice. Cook slowly until mixture coats spoon. Cool. Grease pan with oil. Spread ½ of crumbs. Beat egg whites stiffly. Fold into whipped topping; then into custard. Pour into 9 by 13-inch pan. Top with remaining crumbs. Freeze until firm. Yield: Serves 18.

APPLE GOODIE

2 quarts peeled and chopped
  apples
2½ tablespoons cinnamon
¼ cup sugar
2 cups brown sugar

2 cups oatmeal
2½ teaspoons soda
1¼ cups flour
1¼ cups butter

Place apples in buttered pan and cover with sugar and cinnamon. Mix brown sugar, oatmeal, soda, flour, and butter. Sprinkle brown sugar mixture over apples. Bake in 325° oven for about 30 minutes or until apples are tender. Yield: Serves 10.

APPLE DUMPLINGS

3 quarts peeled and cut apples
6 cups sugar
3½ teaspoons cinnamon
2 sticks butter

2 quarts water
⅓ cup vinegar
1½ teaspoons cloves
pastry

Roll pastry and cut into squares. Put apples in squares and top with 1 teaspoon sugar, dot of butter and sprinkle with cinnamon. Pinch edges together and seal. Put in greased cobbler pan. Mix together water, vinegar, the remaining 4 cups of sugar, 3 teaspoons of cinnamon, and cloves and boil gently for 5 minutes. Pour hot liquid around dumplings and bake in 375° oven for 45 minutes. Yield: Serves 12.

PASTRY FOR APPLE DUMPLINGS

4 cups flour
2 cups shortening
1 heaping teaspoon salt

1⅛ cups ice water
1 teaspoon vinegar

Mix together flour, shortening and salt until crumbles. Add ice water and vinegar only enough to mix together well. Handle as little as possible. Make ahead of time and refrigerate overnight. Let come to room temperature before rolling. Leftover pastry can be frozen.

MAM-MAW'S BOILED CUSTARD

6 egg yolks	pinch of salt
2 cups half and half	½ teaspoon vanilla
¼ cup sugar	

Mix milk, sugar and salt together in *heavy* boiler. Scald (do not boil). Pour milk mixture into slightly beaten egg yolks and stir thoroughly. Pour back into boiler and cook over medium heat for 5 minutes (no longer than 7 minutes) or until mixture coats spoon. Stir constantly. Cool (about 45 minutes). Add vanilla. Stir well. Strain. Pour into pitcher and put in refrigerator. Yield: Serves 4.

This was my grandmother's recipe. In trying to make it through the years, it never looked exactly like hers. One day it dawned on me she always "saved the cream" for her boiled custard. For those of you too young to know what that means, let me explain that before we bought homogenized milk, we bought whole. The cream rose to the top of the container and if you needed whipping cream, you just skimmed the cream off the top. If not, you just shook the milk bottle and had regular milk. When I realized this is what Mam-Maw had done, I tried half and half and it worked!

For special occasions like family reunions or church suppers, she always poured the custard in a punch bowl. She whipped another half cup of cream and placed dabs on top of custard. This was called "floating islands"!

INEZ' MINIATURE CHEESE CAKES

2 8-ounce cream cheese
3 eggs
¾ cup sugar
3 cups graham cracker crumbs

¾ cup sour cream
2 tablespoons granulated sugar
½ teaspoon vanilla

Mix sugar, cheese and beaten egg yolks until light and fluffy. Fold in beaten egg whites. Butter miniature tins generously. Take 1 teaspoon graham cracker crumbs and sift in tins. Cover tins with waxed paper and shake real well. Fill tins ¾ full and bake 15 to 20 minutes at 350⁰. Remove from tin while warm. They will have an indentation. Mix together sour cream, granulated sugar and vanilla in small baking dish and bake at 400⁰ for 5 minutes. Put half teaspoon on each cake in center. Freeze. Yield: 48 miniature cakes.

TWIG'S SWEDISH CREAM

2½ cups whipping cream
1 cup sugar
1 tablespoon gelatin

1 pint sour cream
1 teaspoon vanilla
mixed frozen fruit

Put whipping cream, sugar and gelatin into heavy boiler and heat over *low* heat stirring *constantly* until gelatin is dissolved (about 45 minutes). Cool until it begins to thicken. Add sour cream and vanilla. Refrigerate. Serve with sugared fruit: strawberries, raspberries or any kind of frozen mixed fruit. Yield: Serves 8.

IRENE'S LEMON FREEZE

Desserts

1 13-ounce can evaporated milk
1 cup sugar

juice and rind from 3 lemons
½ box vanilla wafers

Chill evaporated milk real well. Whip milk, adding sugar *slowly*. Add lemon juice and rind *slowly*. Crush vanilla wafers. Place half of the crumbs in the bottom of a 9x13 pan. Spread whipped milk over crumbs. Sprinkle remaining crumbs evenly over whipped milk. Freeze until firm. Yield: Serves 8.

BANANA PUDDING

½ pint whipping cream
½ box vanilla wafers
1 cup crushed pineapple
1 egg
½ cup sugar

juice from pineapple
2 tablespoons flour
4 bananas
½ cup coarsely chopped nuts

Place wafers in 8x8 pan. Slice bananas lengthwise thinly and place on wafers. Put pineapple over bananas. Sprinkle with nuts. Repeat a second layer. Combine egg, sugar, juice and flour and cook over low heat, stirring constantly. Pour over banana mixture. Chill several hours. Top with whipped cream. Yield: Serve 8.

ESTELLE'S FRUIT CAKE SQUARES

½ pound brown sugar
1 stick butter
2 eggs
1 cup flour

½ pound crystalized cherries
6 slices crystalized pineapple
1 teaspoon vanilla
1 cup pecan halves

Cream brown sugar with butter. Add eggs, flour and vanilla. Grease pan and flour lightly. Spread pecans over bottom of pan. Spread batter over nuts. Press cherries and pineapple that have been chopped into batter. Mash fruit into top real well. Bake in 350° oven for 30 to 40 minutes. Cool before cutting. Yield: 24.

53

MYRTLE'S SURPRISE

4 packages prepared whipped
  topping
1 large angel food cake
1 1-pound can crushed
  pineapple

1 cup sugar
juice of 1 lemon
2 packages orange-pineapple
  jello
1 cup boiling water

Soften jello with 4 teaspoons cold water. Add sugar and 1 cup boiling water. Stir. Add pineapple and lemon juice. Mix well. Put in refrigerator until almost thickened. Whip 2 packages of dream whip by directions. Fold into jello mixture. Line 9 by 14 inch pyrex dish with wax paper. Crumble half of cake in pan. Spread all jello mixture on this. Crumble half cake on top of mixture. Cover with foil. Set in refrigerator to set overnight. Turn out on tray. Whip other 2 packages whipped topping and ice cake. Yield: Serves 18.

MYRTLE'S CHERRY YUM-YUM

2½ cups graham cracker crumbs
1½ sticks melted margarine
1½ cups sugar
2 cans cherry pie filling

2 boxes dessert topping mix
1 8-ounce package cream
  cheese
1 cup milk

Combine cracker crumbs, ½ cup sugar and margarine. Mix well. Blend cream cheese, 1 cup sugar, dessert topping mix, and cold milk. Spread half of crumb mixture in oblong baking dish. Add half of cream cheese mixture. Spread on cherry pie filling. Add remaining cream cheese mixture. Top with remaining crumbs. Refrigerate several hours. Yield: Serves 18.

PUMPKIN ICE CREAM

½ gallon vanilla ice cream
2 cups pumpkin
1 cup sugar
1 teaspoon cinnamon
1 teaspoon nutmeg
1 teaspoon ginger

½ teaspoon salt
1 cup chopped pecans
ginger snaps
whipped cream
toasted pecans

Blend softened ice cream with pumpkin, add sugar, spices, salt and pecans. Line oblong 14x8 pan with whole ginger snaps and cover with half of ice cream mixture. Allow to set in freezer. Add another layer of ginger snaps and remainder of ice cream mixture. Cover and freeze. Cut in squares to serve, top with whipped cream and one whole toasted pecan. Yield: Serves 18.

CAROLE'S PUMPKIN TORTE

½ cup chopped dates
½ cup chopped pecans
2 tablespoons flour
¼ cup margarine
1 cup brown sugar
⅔ cup cooked pumpkin
1 teaspoon cinnamon

½ teaspoon nutmeg
¼ teaspoon soda
½ teaspoon ginger
1 teaspoon orange flavoring
⅓ cup flour
½ teaspoon baking powder
2 eggs

Mix dates, pecans and 2 tablespoons flour together and set aside. Add all other ingredients together and add to date mixture. Bake in ungreased square dish 25 minutes in 350° oven. Cut in squares and may top with whipping cream. May be frozen after baked. Yield: Serves 10.

MIL'S SOFT GINGERBREAD

¾ cup butter
1½ cups sugar
1½ cups molasses
3 well beaten eggs
4½ cups sifted flour
3 tablespoons soda

3 tablespoons ginger
1 tablespoon cinnamon
1 teaspoon allspice
¾ teaspoon cloves
¾ teaspoon nutmeg
1½ cups buttermilk

Cream butter and sugar. Add molasses and eggs. Mix together other dry ingredients and add buttermilk. Mix well. Pour into greased pan and bake in 350° oven for 30-35 minutes. Yield: Serves 24.

ORANGE SAUCE FOR GINGERBREAD

1½ cups sugar
3 tablespoons cornstarch
½ teaspoon salt
1½ cups orange juice
⅓ cup lemon juice

⅓ cup water
2 egg yolks
1½ tablespoons grated orange
  rind

Mix sugar, cornstarch, salt and orange juice together. Add lemon juice and water. Beat egg yolks and add to other ingredients. Stir in orange rind. Yield: 4 cups.

LOUISE'S BANANA BREAD

¾ cup butter or margarine
1½ cups sugar
1½ cups mashed banana
2 well-beaten eggs
2 cups flour
1 teaspoon soda

¾ teaspoon salt
½ cup buttermilk
1 cup chopped walnuts or
  pecans
1 teaspoon vanilla

Cream butter and sugar. Add mashed bananas. Add rest of ingredients. Bake in 325° oven for approximately 1¼ hours. Yield: 1 large loaf or two small loaves.

MYRTLE'S PUMPKIN BREAD

2½ cups flour
2 cups sugar
2 cups cooked pumpkin
½ cup peanut oil
½ teaspoon cloves

2 teaspoons soda
1 teaspoon cinnamon
½ teaspoon salt
½ teaspoon vanilla
½ cup chopped pecans

Mix all ingredients together. Grease and flour 1-pound coffee cans. Pour batter into 2 cans and bake in preheated 350° oven for 1 hour. Turn off oven and leave in oven for 15 minutes. Turn out of coffee cans on cloth when cool. Yield: Serves 16.

IRENE'S ZUCCHINI WALNUT BREAD

1 cup black walnuts
4 eggs
2 cups sugar
1 cup oil
3½ cups flour
1½ teaspoons soda
1½ teaspoons salt

¾ teaspoon baking powder
2 cups packed grated zucchini
1 cup raisins
1 teaspoon vanilla
1 teaspoon cinnamon
¼ cup brown sugar

Chop walnuts into medium pieces. Beat eggs and gradually add sugar, then oil. Combine dry ingredients, leaving our ½ teaspoon cinnamon. Add to first mixture alternately with zucchini, raisins and walnuts. Reserve ¼ cup walnuts. Add vanilla. Pour into 2 greased and floured loaf pans. Sprinkle brown sugar, remaining ¼ cup walnuts and ½ teaspoon cinnamon on top before baking. Bake on lowest rack in 350° oven for 55 minutes. Let stand 10 minutes. Turn on wire racks to cool. Yield: 2 loaves.

Our
Heavenly Father,
we are so thankful
*   that Thou dost continue*
to watch over us
and care for us.
We pause now
*   to sing Thy praise.*
We lift
our hands and hearts
to Thee for this good day and Thy mercy.
We thank you for Thy love.
We thank you for this food, and the hands that prepared it.
*   In Jesus' name we ask it. Amen.*

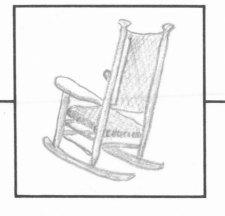

Eggs
& Cheese

EGGS

So many people ask about our scrambled eggs. We do not add milk or cream to them. I think the secret to good scrambled eggs is having the grease hot (again we use peanut oil), beat the eggs well, use a black skillet, and take the eggs off the flame before they look done. They will cook a little more after the heat is off and you have stirred some more. You must stir constantly.

We use for a full house (60 people):

90 well beaten eggs
2 large black skillets
approximately ½ cup peanut oil
   for each skillet

salt and pepper to taste at table
as so many people are leaving
off salt

On poached egg morning, we have egg poachers and cook soft, medium and hard. Nathalie Dupree says "add a small amount of water to make eggs fluffy" in scrambled eggs or omelets. We add about ¼ cup to 90 eggs.

HEMLOCK INN GRITS

1 cup coarse ground grits   **½ teaspoon salt**
4 cups water

Pour water into heavy boiler and add salt. Bring water to boil and add grits. Immediately turn heat down to very slow cooking. Stir very often since grits stick easily. Cook for about 45 minutes. Yield: Serves 10.

We have to have our grits ground special for our purpose. Jim Dandy used to grind them for us, but since the company was sold, it is not possible to get coarse-ground grits anymore. They tell us "the whole world has gone instant"—although we don't believe them, we can't do anything about it. We have found a miller in a little town in north Georgia that grinds our grits for us now! You may buy a package when you come for a visit!!

LUCILLE'S SAUSAGE EGG SOUFFLE

6 eggs   **1 teaspoon salt**
2 cups milk   **1 teaspoon dry mustard**
6 slices white bread   **1 pound mild sausage**
1 cup cheddar cheese

Crumble and brown sausage. Drain and cool. Mix eggs, milk, salt, dry mustard, and add to cheese after grating and bread after cubing. Add to sausage and pour into 9x13-inch casserole and refrigerate overnight. Bake for 45 minutes in 350° oven. Yield: Serves 6.

HEMLOCK INN CHEESE GRITS

2 cups cooked coarse ground grits

½ cup grated sharp cheese
¼ cup melted margarine

Mix grits with cheese real well. Stir in melted margarine. Put in 1½ quart oblong casserole and bake in 350° oven for about 20 minutes or until cheese melts and is hot. Yield: Serves 10.

GRITS SOUFFLE

1½ cups quick grits
6 cups unsalted water
1 pound grated cheddar cheese
1½ sticks margarine

3 teaspoons seasoned salt
3 eggs
1½ teaspoons tabasco

Cook grits in water. Add cheese, margarine, salt and tabasco. Beat eggs well and add to grits mixture. Bake in 325° oven for 1 hour. Can be made ahead and frozen. Yield: Serves 10.

CHEESE STRATA

2 eggs
2½ cups milk
12 slices white bread

pinch of salt
pinch of pepper
¾ pound grated sharp cheese

Grease a casserole with margarine. Cut off sides of bread and place in bottom of casserole. Completely cover with grated cheese. Cover with another layer of bread. Beat together eggs, milk, salt and pepper. Pour over top of bread and cheese in casserole, letting soak through. Put in refrigerator overnight. Bake in 325° oven for about 1 hour. Bake until puffy. Yield: Serves 10.

HEMLOCK INN PIMENTO CHEESE

1 1-pound sharp cheddar cheese
1 4-ounce jar pimentos

½ cup mayonnaise
pinch of salt

Let cheese stand at room temperature for about 2 hours. Cut into cubes. Cut pimentos in pieces. Mix cheese, pimentos, mayonnaise and salt in mixing bowl. At medium speed in electric mixer, mix until consistency for easy spreading. More mayonnaise may added if needed to spread easier. Yield: 4 cups.

Our Heavenly
   Father,
we do hunger and thirst
   after righteousness
and our prayer is that Thou
would fill our hearts.
We come now to receive Thy grace,
and we thank Thee for Thy continued mercy. We thank Thee
   for a new day, for Thy strength, and now for this food.
                    In Jesus' blessed name we ask it. Amen.

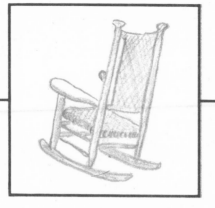

Poultry

FRYING CHICKEN FLOUR

3 cups flour
3 teaspoons paprika
1 teaspoon accent

4 teaspoons salt
1 teaspoon pepper

Mix all together and put in paper bag. Shake damp chicken in bag. Place in black skillet with about ¼ inch of peanut oil. Can be used several times if kept in air-tight container.

CHICKEN LIVERS

Chicken livers must be of good quality and fresh. (May be frozen, not old!) Salt and pepper to taste and put small amount of flour on them. Cover with peanut oil hot (350º) in deep fryer and cook until well done. They must be done, but not crisp. They need to be juicy, not dry. Remove from fryer and drain well on rack. Serve piping hot.

CHICKEN GRAVY

Leave ¼ cup hot grease in black skillet after frying chicken. Add 3 tablespoons flour and stir constantly over medium heat until base begins to brown. Slowly add 3 cups milk and stir with whisk until thickens. Yield: 2 cups.

CHICKEN AND DUMPLINGS

Poultry

2 large baking hens   1 tablespoon salt

Put hens in large pot and cover with salted water. (We use 16-quart aluminum pot.) Bring to boil, cover and turn heat down to low. Cook for approximately 3 hours, or until chicken falls off the bone easily. Remove hens from the water, drain, remove all bones and skin and set aside.

2 cups self-rising flour   2 tablespoons flour
¼ cup peanut oil   salt and pepper to taste
1 egg   poultry seasoning if desired
½ cup milk

Mix all ingredients together in mixing bowl until soft dough is formed. Turn out on board. Kneed to rolling consistency. Roll out approximately ⅛ inch thick and cut into strips and cut into 3-inch pieces. For thickening, gradually stir 2 tablespoons flour into broth from cooking chickens and bring to rolling boil. Add salt and pepper to taste. You can add poultry seasoning but be careful not to get too strong. Cut broth mixture down to simmer and drop 3-inch dumplings into pot and cook for approximately 10 minutes. Dip dumplings along with some of the thickened broth onto a deep platter. Place pieces of chicken around the outside of the platter. Yield: Serves 20.

HEMLOCK DRESSING

2 cups chopped celery   ¼ teaspoon pepper
1 cup chicken fat   1 teaspoon poultry seasoning
1¼ cups chopped onions   ½ teaspoon accent
1 quart crumbled cornbread   1½ quarts chicken broth
3 cups large dry bread crumbs   4 beaten eggs
2 teaspoons salt

Sauté celery and onions in fat until celery is tender but not brown. Mix together the bread crumbs, salt, pepper, poultry seasoning, accent, and chicken broth. Allow crumbs to soften. Add eggs to bread mixture. Add celery and onions. Turn into buttered pan and bake in 400° oven for about 30 minutes. Yield: Serves 12.

ANNETTE'S CHICKEN SALAD

1 4 or 5 pound hen
1 large onion
3 stalks celery
1 teaspoon salt
¼ teaspoon black pepper
12 pieces of white or light pickle

4 hard boiled eggs
3 cups mayonnaise
2 cups of white seedless grapes
½ pound slivered almonds
12 slices pineapple
12 leaves of lettuce

Cook chicken and remove bones. Cut into small pieces. Chop 2 cups celery (using only tender parts). Mix together with seasoning, pickles, eggs, almonds, grapes (cut in halves) and mayonnaise. Let stand in refrigerator about an hour. Serve on slice of pineapple which has been placed on crisp lettuce leaf. Yield: Serves 12.

MILLIE'S HOT CHICKEN SALAD

2 cups diced cooked chicken
1 cup cream of chicken soup
1 cup diced celery
¼ teaspoon pepper
1 tablespoon lemon juice
¾ cup mayonnaise

2 teaspoons minced onions
½ cup chopped English walnuts
½ teaspoon salt
3 hard cooked thinly sliced eggs
2 cups crushed potato chips
parsley

Combine all ingredients except potato chips. Pour into 8x12-inch pan. Top with crushed potato chips. Bake in 350° oven for 20 minutes. Garnish with parsley. Yield: Serves 8.

CHICKEN PIE

2 cups diced cooked chicken
3 cups chicken broth
3 tablespoons flour

½ teaspoon salt
⅛ teaspoon pepper
Pie Crust

Cut chicken in bite size pieces. We use leftover chicken that has been frozen or cooked chicken parts such as wings, backs and pieces that we don't use for frying. Put chicken in shallow pyrex dish. Mix salt, pepper, flour and broth together. If you don't have broth from a cooked chicken, you can make broth by using 1½ heaping tablespoons chicken soup base and 3 cups water. Pour broth over chicken. Cover with pastry and bake in 375° oven for 45 mintutes or until crust is golden brown. Use pie crust recipe in this book. It may be made ahead and frozen. Yield: Serves 10.

SISTER JEANNE'S CHICKEN

8 boned chicken breast halves
1 16-ounce jar dried beef
4 slices bacon

1 8-ounce carton sour cream
1 can undiluted mushroom soup

Salt and pepper chicken breasts. Wrap 2 pieces of dried beef around chicken. Cut bacon in two halves. Wrap half slice bacon around chicken and hold together with toothpick. Mix sour cream and soup together. Spoon on top of chicken. Bake uncovered in 275° oven for 2½ to 3 hours. Yield: Serves 8.

Our Heavenly Father,
  we come to Thee in
the powerful and holy name of Jesus.
We come lifting our hands and hearts
  to Thee in praise.
We are so thankful Thou dost love us and care for us.
We thank Thee for this beautiful day, and for Thy mercy,
for these friends and now for this food.
In Jesus' blessed name we ask it. Amen.

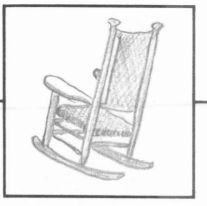

Pork

COUNTRY HAM

The secret to good country ham is not only how it is cooked, but where it is cured. We buy all of our hams at this time direct from the curing place in Smithfield, Virginia. Our local market stopped selling the hams we liked best so we were able to make a connection with the Virginia people. We have tried others in the past, but find none compare to these. We have the ham sliced the day before we use it. It is then trimmed, leaving only a small amount of fat and most all bones are removed. A small amount of oil is put in a black skillet and heated until drop of water in skillet bubbles. The pieces of country ham are then placed in the skillet and cooked at medium heat *only* until slightly brown. Most people overcook good ham—it's already cured, you just want to make it tasty!

RED EYE GRAVY

¼ cup ham grease   2 cups strong black coffee

After you have fried your country ham, pour off excess grease and leave ¼ cup grease in black skillet. While still hot pour in coffee and simmer for 2-3 minutes. Yield: 2 cups.

CAROLYN'S SAUSAGE RICE

½ cup plain long grain rice   2 or 3 stalks celery
1 box chicken noodle soup   ¼ cup onion
4½ cups broth of chicken   ¼ cup bell pepper
½ cup slivered almonds   1 pound sausage

Cook rice, chicken noodle soup and broth for 7 minutes. You can use canned chicken broth. Saute celery, onion, bell pepper in oil or margarine and add to soup mixture. Cook sausage; drain and crumble. Mix sausage to soup and rice mixture. Add almonds, if desired. Bake in casserole dish in 350⁰ oven for 1 hour. This freezes well. Yield: Serves 6 to 8.

BACON

The question is asked so often: "How do you get your bacon so straight?" John's answer is: "We iron it?" The truth is, we cook our bacon in a 350° oven stacked on racks that have been placed in a pan to collect the grease. Bacon is laid on cake-cooling racks that fit into shallow baking pan. In cooking 1 pound of bacon, lay no more than 9 pieces on each rack (do not let pieces touch). Stack racks one on the other. The drippings will have to be drained several times during cooking. It is taken out of the oven and wiped with a paper towel to remove excess grease. We buy only top grade breakfast bacon.

STREAK-O-LEAN

We buy the best of streak-o-lean, or fatback, or salt pork, or whatever you call it in your part of the country. It is sliced very thin and placed in sugar water the night before we serve the next day. Small amount of sugar—approximately 1 teaspoon to 2 quarts of water. The morning of serving, the streak-o-lean is drained well, dipped in a *small* amount of flour, and fried very slowly in hot peanut oil that barely covers the meat. The streak-o-lean is fried until golden crisp. It has been called: Georgia Chicken, Sawmill Chicken, Tennessee Chicken, Bryson City T-Bone, Country Bacon, or you may call it something else; but when served with country gravy it surely is popular!

Pour off all but about ½ cup grease. Stir in 2 tablespoons of flour and stir constantly until brown. Slowly add about 1½ to 2 cups milk to flour mixture and stir constantly until thick as desired. We do not add salt because grease will be pretty salty—you may add if you want. Yield: 1½-2 cups.

E.J.'S PORK CHOP DISH

4 1-inch center cut pork chops
1 medium onion
1 bell pepper
1 teaspoon salt
⅛ teaspoon pepper
4 heaping teaspoons uncooked rice
1 1-pound can whole tomatoes

Put pork chops in 1½ quart casserole. Put slice of onion and slice of bell pepper on each pork chop. Place 1 heaping teaspoon of rice in middle of each pork chop. Sprinkle salt and pepper all over. Put ½ cup tomatoes on each pork chop. Put aluminum foil over and bake in 350° oven for 1 hour. Yield: Serves 4.

Our
*   Heavenly Father,*
we thank Thee
*   for Thy watchcare, and*
we thank Thee
*   for Thy guidance.*
We thank Thee for this lovely day,
for good friends, and Thy continued mercy.
We are especially thankful for times when we might wait on Thee.
We have felt Thy presence this day, and for this we are so grateful.
Thank you now for this food.   In Jesus' name we ask it. Amen.

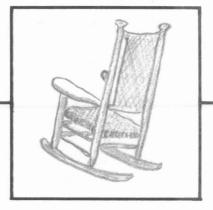

Beef

BARBECUED BEEF BALLS

1 pound ground beef
1 teaspoon accent
⅔ teaspoon salt

1 tablespoon chopped onion
½ cup bread crumbs
¼ cup milk

Mix beef, accent, salt, and onions together. Soak bread crumbs in milk for 10 minutes. Add to beef mixture. Make meat balls and roll in small amount of flour. Brown quickly. Do not cook done. Cover with sauce below and simmer in 350º oven for 20 minutes.

2 tablespoons molasses
¼ cup vinegar
¼ cup catsup

¼ teaspoon Tabasco
¼ teaspoon oregano

Yield: Makes approximately 14 small balls.

COUNTRY FRIED STEAK

1½ pounds round cubed steak
1 teaspoon salt
⅛ teaspoon pepper

½ cup flour
½ cup peanut oil

The secret of all good meat is to buy only prime or choice meat. And be sure you have a dependable meat market. Mix salt, pepper and flour together. Have grease hot. Dip steak into flour mixture and brown well on both sides in black skillet. Remove from heat and place steak in blue enamel roaster pan with rack in bottom to keep from sticking. Pour left-over flour mixture into black skillet, brown, add water to make gravy. Gravy ratio is always: 1 tablespoon flour, ¼ teaspoon salt, pinch of pepper to 1 cup liquid. Make as much gravy as needed to slightly cover steak. Place covered blue roaster in 375º oven for 1½ hours. Yield: Serves 6.

MIL'S SPAGHETTI SAUCE

1 pound ground beef
1 can tomato paste
1 can tomato sauce
½ cup finely chopped onion
1½ cups water
2 teaspoons brown gravy mix
fresh crushed garlic bud
2 teaspoons Worcestershire
   sauce

2 teaspoons sugar
1 teaspoon oregano
1 teaspoon basil
½ teaspoon salt
½ teaspoon pepper
parmesan cheese

Saute beef and add to other ingredients. Simmer very slowly in open kettle for 1½ to 2 hours. Stir often. Yield: Serves 8.

GEORGIA'S SPAGHETTI SAUCE

1 tablespoon peanut oil
1 tablespoon onion
1 pound ground meat
2 cups tomato sauce
1 cup tomato paste

1 teaspoon salt
1 teaspoon pepper
1 tablespoon Worcestershire
1 tablespoon brown gravy sauce
1 garlic bud or garlic salt

Brown onion in oil. Add ground meat and cook but don't brown. Put meat and onion mixture in large pot and add tomato sauce and tomato paste. Add salt, pepper, Worcestershire and brown gravy sauce and garlic. Simmer on low heat for at least 3 hours. Yield: Serves 10.

ALMA'S STUFFED GREEN PEPPERS

8 green peppers
6 tablespoons chopped onion
½ cup margarine
1 teaspoon poultry seasoning
1½ cups cooked rice

1 pound ground beef
½ teaspoon salt
¼ teaspoon black pepper
1 8-ounce can tomato sauce

Wash peppers; cut into half from stem end. Remove seeds. Cover with boiling water (slightly salted), boil uncovered for 3 to 5 minutes. Drain. Brown onion in margarine and add ground beef. Add poultry seasoning, rice, salt and pepper. Add tomato sauce to this meat and rice mixture. Fill peppers with mixture and place in baking dish. Bake in 400° oven for 15 to 20 minutes. Yield: Serves 12.

BLUE CHEESE TURNOVERS

2 tablespoons bacon fat
2 medium chopped onions
1 pound lean ground beef
½ cup bread crumbs
½ teaspoon dry mustard
¼ teaspoon garlic salt

¼ teaspoon basil
¼ teaspoon paprika
1 tablespoon Worcestershire
   sauce
½ cup crumbled blue cheese

Brown onions in fat slightly. Add beef to onions and brown. Mix crumbs, mustard, garlic salt, basil and paprika to meat mixture and cook a few minutes. Cool. Add blue cheese to mixture and mix well. Put tablespoon of mixture into 4-inch pastry squares, fold and seal, like an apple tart. Bake in 375° oven for 15 minutes or until brown. Yield: 24.

We use our pastry recipe anytime pastry is mentioned in a recipe.

BEEF PIE

2 cups beef
3 cups beef broth
3 tablespoons flour

½ teaspoon salt
⅛ teaspoon pepper
Pie Crust

Cut beef in bite size pieces. We use leftover from our beef roasts—we use only choice or prime beef; so be sure pieces of beef are tender. Put beef in shallow pyrex dish. Mix salt, pepper, flour and broth together. If you don't have broth from your beef roast, you can make broth by using 2 heaping tablespoons beef soup base and 3 cups water. Pour broth over beef. Cover with pastry and bake in 375° oven for 45 minutes or until crust is golden brown. Use Pie Crust recipe in this book. It may be made ahead and frozen. Yield: Serves 10.

EGGPLANT PARMESAN

2 large eggplants
2 cups bread crumbs
½ teaspoon oregano
½ teaspoon garlic powder
½ teaspoon salt

¼ teaspoon pepper
4 to 6 cups spaghetti sauce
¼ cup grated parmesan cheese
1 cup grated mozzarella cheese

Wash, drain and peel eggplants. Slice into 1-inch pieces. Mix bread crumbs, oregano, garlic powder, salt and pepper together. Roll eggplant pieces in bread crumb mixture. Place on oiled baking tray and put in 400° oven for about 20 minutes. In 9x13-inch casserole, pour a small amount of spaghetti sauce—just enough to cover bottom and to keep eggplant from sticking. (We use Mil's Spaghetti Sauce recipe found in meat section.) Put pieces of eggplant over spaghetti sauce. Pour layer of spaghetti sauce on top of eggplant. Sprinkle half of parmesan and mozarella cheese on top of spaghetti sauce. Repeat eggplant, spaghetti sauce and cheeses once more, ending with the cheeses as topping. Bake in 350° oven for 30 to 45 minutes or until bubbly and cheese is melted. Yield: Serves 10.

79

CORNED BEEF HASH

2 cups cooked corned beef	2 pounds potatoes
1⅓ cups hot water	¾ cup ground onions
2 slightly rounded tablespoons beef flavor	

Grate finely potatoes and mix with onions and corned beef. Put broth (hot water and beef flavor) over mixture. Place in covered pan (we use blue enamel roaster) in 350° oven for about 1 hour or until potatoes are done. When ready to serve, warm in casserole and serve hot. Yield: Serves 12.

EYE OF ROUND

Have eye of the round roast at room temperature. Sprinkle with coarse black pepper or other seasoning. Preheat oven to 500°. Bake 5 minutes per pound. Turn off and do not open oven for 2 hours. Roast will be pink.

BEEF GRAVY

Pour hot juices from cooking beef roast into skillet—about 1 cup. Add ¼ cup flour slowly, stirring constantly over medium heat. Whisk until well blended. Add 3 cups water and cook slowly until brown and thickens. Yield: 2 cups.

HEMLOCK INN MEAT LOAF

3 pounds ground beef
½ cup catsup
1 cup chopped onions
6 eggs
1 teaspoon salt

1 tablespoon Worcestershire
  sauce
⅔ cup bread crumbs
⅔ cup stewed tomatoes
4 tablespoons butter (optional)

Mix all ingredients together and put in greased baking pan. Bake in 350°
oven for 1 hour. Yield: Serves 20.

CORNBREAD MEAT LOAF

1 pound ground beef
½ pound sausage
1 egg
1 cup cornbread crumbs
1 chopped onion
1½ teaspoon salt

¼ teaspoon pepper
1 cup tomato sauce
1 cup water
2 tablespoons vinegar
2 tablespoons mustard
2 tablespoons brown sugar

Mix ground beef, sausage, egg, cornbread crumbs, onion, salt, pepper
and ½ cup tomato sauce. Mold into mound and put in greased baking
dish. Combine water, vinegar, ½ cup tomato sauce, mustard and brown
sugar. Pour over meat loaf. Bake in 325° oven for about 45 minutes. Baste
several times while baking. Yield: Serves 6.

Our Heavenly Father,
  we would truly come to Thee
as this new day starts,
  and pray
that Thou would somehow
draw us close to Thee and lift us
  to a loftier level.
We thank Thee for Thy strength, and now for this food.
                              In Jesus' name we ask it. Amen.

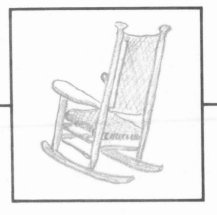

Seafood

CORNELIA'S TUNA SALAD

1 8-ounce can tuna fish
1 cup chopped celery
2 cups grated carrots
2 small chopped onions
1 cup mayonnaise

1 cup chopped stuffed olives
1 cup chopped cashews
1 cup chow mein noodles
3 hard boiled eggs

Mix tuna, celery, carrots, onions, mayonnaise, olives, and eggs together and put in refrigerator until ready to serve. Toss cashews and noodles into the tuna mixture just before serving. Yield: Serves 8.

THELMA'S TUNA MACARONI CASSEROLE

1 cup uncooked macaroni
1 7-ounce can solid pack white
   tuna
¼ pound sharp grated cheese
1 heaping teaspoon prepared
   mustard

1 teaspoon Worcestershire
   sauce
1 heaping tablespoon finely
   chopped onion

Cook macaroni, drain, and let set in cold water for 10 minutes. Sauté onions slightly. Make sauce with:

2 tablespoons margarine
¼ cup flour

1¼ cup milk
¼ teaspoon salt

Add Worcestershire sauce, mustard, and chopped onion. Add cheese to sauce mixture and stir until blended. Break up tuna and add to sauce. Mix drained macaroni, put in casserole, and bake in 325° oven for 45 minutes. You can sprinkle top with bread crumbs, dot with butter and add paprika to make look pretty. Yield: Serves 8.

MILDRED'S BAKED FISH

½ cup mayonnaise
¼ cup prepared mustard
½ lemon
½ teaspoon salt
¼ teaspoon paprika

¼ teaspoon garlic salt
1 teaspoon pepper
1 pound package frozen cod
    fillets

Mix together mayonnaise, mustard, juice from lemon, salt, paprika, garlic salt and pepper. Cut cod fish into 2-inch squares and put in greased 1½ quart casserole. Pour mayonnaise mixture over fish. Bake in 350° oven for 30 to 45 minutes. Yield: Serves 8.

In our kitchen, we partially thaw frozen package of cod fish. *Do not separate fish;* but cut into 2-inch squares the depth of the frozen cod fish package.

EASY TUNA CASSEROLE

1 8-ounce package noodles
1 7-ounce can tuna fish
½ cup mayonnaise
¼ cup minced onion

1 teaspoon salt
1 cup cream of celery soup
½ cup milk
½ cup grated sharp cheese

Heat together mayonnaise, onion, salt, soup, milk, and cheese. Cook noodles, drain and put in baking dish. Add tuna to heated sauce mixture. Pour mixture over noodles. Bake in 425° oven for 20 minutes. Yield: Serves 8.

MARY'S TUNA BAKE

1 8-ounce can white flaked tuna
1 10-ounce can cream of
    mushroom soup

1 2-ounce package potato chips

Drain tuna real well and mix together with soup. Crush potato chips and mix in tuna mixture. Put in baking dish and bake in 350° oven for about 30 minutes. Yield: Serves 4.

PAT'S TUNA BAKE

1 egg
½ cup uncooked instant rice
1½ cup grated sharp cheese
1 14-ounce can drained tuna fish
½ cup sliced stuffed olives
2 tablespoons parsley
1 tablespoon instant minced
  onion

2 teaspoons mustard
1 teaspoon salt
1 dash pepper
1 13-ounce can evaporated milk
½ cup water

In ungreased 2-quart casserole, beat egg slightly; mix in rice, ¾ of cheese, tuna fish, olives, and seasonings. Stir in milk and water. Sprinkle remaining cheese on top. Cover and bake in 350⁰ oven for 40 minutes. Yield: Serves 10.

BOBBYE'S SHRIMP AND CHICKEN CREOLE

1 medium onion
3 cloves garlic
1½ cups pre-cooked rice
½ cup bell pepper
¼ cup butter or margarine
¾ cup sharp cheese
1 can tomatoes

1 teaspoon salt
dash cayenne pepper
2 5 or 6-ounce cans boned
  chicken
2 4 or 5-ounce cans shrimp
¼ pound sliced sharp cheese

Grate onion and sauté with bell pepper, garlic, and rice in butter or margarine for 3 to 5 minutes. Add tomatoes, salt, and cayenne pepper. Mix well. Cut chicken in bite size pieces and add liquid from chicken. Drain shrimp and add. Put half of mixture in casserole and sprinkle grated cheese over it. Add rest of mixture. Cover and bake in pre-heated oven 350⁰ for 20 to 25 minutes. Remove from oven and arrange 1 inch wide strips of cheese over top and return to oven 2 to 3 minutes to melt slightly. Yield: Serves 8.

BARBARA'S SALMON LOAF

1 1-pound can salmon	2 eggs
1 can cream of celery soup	½ cup chopped onions
1 cup bread crumbs	1 tablespoons lemon juice

Mix all ingredients together real well. Grease loaf pan and line with waxed paper. Pour ingredients in pan. Bake in 375° oven for 1 hour. Cool 10 minutes. Turn out and serve. Yield: Serves 8.

SEA FOOD SALAD

1 3-ounce package lemon jello	2 tablespoons horseradish
1 cup boiling water	1 cup canned or cooked shrimp
½ cup chili sauce	1 cup canned or cooked crab
1 tablespoon vinegar	claw meat
3 drops tabasco	1 cup chopped celery
1 teaspoon Worcestershire	1 cup bell pepper
sauce	pinch of salt.

Dissolve jello in boiling water. Mix sauce, vinegar, tabasco, Worcestershire and horseradish together in measuring cup. Add cold water to ingredients to make 1 cup of liquid. Add jello mixture. Let set until it starts to set. Add celery, bell pepper, salt and seafood. Let jell. Yield: Serves 8.

Wonderful for luncheon.

Our Heavenly Father,
   we come seeking Thee this morning,
and we come praying
for Thy continued mercy. We pray
   that we might somehow be like Thee,
and walk with Thee this day. We thank thee
for Thy strength, and for this food.

                    In Jesus' name we ask it. Amen.

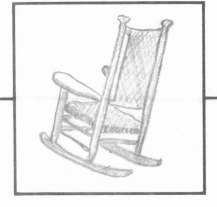

Pies
& Pastries

PIE CRUST

5 cups flour
2½ cups shortening
½ teaspoon salt

1 egg
2 teaspoons vinegar

Beat 1 egg in cup. Add 2 teaspoons vinegar. Fill cup with water to make one full cup. Stir to break egg yolk. Add to flour mixture all at once and mix. Divide into 6 balls. Put unused portions in freezer. Yield: 6 single crusts.

Note: We find if you bake *slightly* your pie shell even though you pour pie filling into unbaked shell, the pie will not be soggy!

EASY MERINGUE

4 egg whites at room
   temperature

¼ teaspoon cream of tartar
½ cup sugar

Beat egg whites and cream of tartar until foamy. Beat in sugar gradually. Beat until meringue forms stiff glossy peaks. Swirl on cooled filling with spoon or spatula. Seal against crust edge to prevent shrinkage. Bake in preheated oven at 450° for 10 to 15 minutes or until meringue is brown-tipped.

QUAKER PIE

⅔ cup sugar
2 beaten eggs
⅔ cup uncooked oatmeal
½ cup light corn syrup

⅔ cup melted margarine
¼ teaspoon salt
1 teaspoon vanilla

Mix all ingredients together. Pour into unbaked pie shell. Bake in 350⁰ oven for 1 hour. Yield: 1 pie.

HELEN'S CHESS PIE

3 eggs
1 cup sugar
½ cup brown sugar
1 tablespoon corn meal
1 tablespoon flour

1 stick melted margarine
1 teaspoon vinegar
1 teaspoon vanilla
pinch of nutmeg if desired
1 uncooked pie shell

Preheat oven to 375⁰. Cream eggs and mix with sugar and corn meal. Add flour and melted margarine. Stir in vinegar, vanilla and nutmeg if desired. Pour into unbaked pie shell and bake 10 minutes. Cut down heat to 325⁰ and bake 35 minutes. Yield: 1 pie.

There's an old story told in the South about the origin of Chess Pie. At a church "dinner-on-the-ground" meeting, someone brought a delicious new pie that no one had tasted before. When asked what kind of pie, the baker answered: "Oh, it's jus' pie". Not understanding the Southern drawl too well, the visitor thought she said Chess Pie... No, it isn't "a weed, floor planks or skilled game" as listed under chess in Mr. Webster's dictionary! — It's jus' pie! (It may not be true, but it happens so often here in our mountains that it could easily be a true story!)

CHOCOLATE CHESS PIE

1½ cups sugar
3 tablespoons cocoa
2 eggs
½ stick melted butter

1 6-ounce can evaporated milk
1 teaspoon vanilla
1 unbaked pie shell

Mix all ingredients together and pour into thawed pie shell. Bake for 1 hour at 350⁰. Yield: 1 pie.

HEMLOCK INN CHOCOLATE PIE

2 egg yolks
1 cup milk
1 cup sugar
½ stick margarine

2 heaping tablespoons flour
2 heaping tablespoons cocoa
1 teaspoon vanilla
1 9-inch baked pie shell

Beat egg yolks slightly. Add sugar, milk, margarine, flour, cocoa and cook over medium heat stirring constantly until thick. Add vanilla. Pour into baked pie shell. Use egg whites to make meringue. Yield: Serves 8.

STRAWBERRY PIE

3 heaping tablespoons
strawberry jello
3 heaping tablespoons
cornstarch

1 cup sugar
1 cup very warm water
1 pint strawberries
1 baked pie shell

Bake pie shell. Set aside to cool. Cook jello, cornstarch, sugar and water until thick. Set aside. Slice strawberries and drain well. Put strawberries into pie shell. Pour mixture over berries. Chill. May top with dab of whipped cream. Yield: 1 pie.

DODY'S BANANA SPLIT PIE

3 bananas
1 tablespoon lemon juice
1 9-inch graham cracker crust
1 pint strawberry ice cream
1 cup whipped topping

1 8-ounce jar whole maraschino
cherries
2 tablespoons finely chopped
nuts

Slice bananas thinly sprinkled with lemon juice and arrange on bottom of pie crust. Stir ice cream to soften slightly—spread over bananas. Freeze. Spread thawed whipped topping over ice cream. Top with cherries. Sprinkle with nuts. Freeze again. Let stand 30 minutes at room temperature before serving. Pour Chocolate Quick Sauce over each serving. Yield: Serves 8.

CHOCOLATE QUICK SAUCE

1 package 6-ounce chocolate
chips

$2/3$ cup evaporated milk
1 cup marshmallow creme

Cook chocolate chips, milk together over low heat. Beat or in marshmallow creme until blended. Serve warm or cold.

93

VELDA'S OLD FASHIONED LEMON PIE

¼ cup softened margarine
2 cups sugar
4 eggs

2 lemons with juice and rind
1 unbaked pie shell

Cream margarine and sugar; add eggs, one at at time, beating well after each addition. Stir in lemon juice and rind; mix well. Pour into unbaked pie shell. Bake at 350° for 40 minutes or until set and lightly browned. Yield: 1 pie.

MRS. GARRETT'S FROZEN LEMON PIE

⅔ cup sugar
pinch of salt
3 egg yolks
¼ cup lemon juice
1 tablespoon grated lemon rind

3 egg whites
1 cup evaporated milk
1 baked pie shell
¼ cup graham cracker
    crumbs

Mix sugar, salt, egg yolks, lemon juice and rind together and cook in heavy boiler for 15 minutes. *Will not thicken.* Cool. Beat egg whites until stiff and fold into cooked mixture. Whip *ice cold* evaporated milk until stiff and fold into the cooked mixture. Pour into baked pie shell, cover with graham cracker crumbs and freeze. Yield: 1 large pie.

MIL'S LEMON MERINGUE PIE

2½ cups water
2 cups sugar
5 heaping tablespoons
   cornstarch
3 eggs

⅛ teaspoon salt
¼ stick butter or margarine
juice of 3 lemons
grated rind of 2 lemons
2 baked pie shells

Mix 2 cups water and sugar together and bring to boil. Mix cornstarch, ½ cup water, 3 egg *yolks,* salt real well and add to sugar and water mixture. Stir constantly until thickens. Add butter, lemon juice and rind. Pour into baked pie shells. Beat egg whites until stiff and put on top of pies. You may want to sprinkle a small amount of powdered sugar in egg whites just before they get stiff. We use the easy meringue recipe in this section. Bake in 375° oven for 10 to 12 minutes or until as brown as you like your pie to look. Yield: 2 pies.

PINEAPPLE CREAM PIE

1 8-ounce cream cheese
1 can condensed milk
½ cup lemon juice
1 1-pound cool whip

1 20-ounce can crushed
   pineapple
2 baked pie shells

Cream together cream cheese, condensed milk; and add lemon juice. Drain pineapple real well. Add to cool whip. Fold into cream cheese mixture. Pour into baked pie shells. Yield: 2 pies.

COCONUT CREAM PIE

2 cups milk
2 cups sugar
½ cup shredded coconut
5 heaping tablespoons
   cornstarch
½ cup evaporated milk

3 egg yolks
⅛ teaspoon salt
¼ stick butter or margarine
1 teaspoon vanilla
2 baked pie shells

Mix together milk, sugar and cornstarch and bring to boil. Beat egg yolks
and add evaporated milk. Add to milk mixture. Stirring constantly, cook
until thick. Add salt, butter, vanilla and coconut. Stir until melted and
blended. Pour into baked pie shells and let cool. Top with *Easy Meringue.*
Yield: Serves 16. 2 pies.

MIL'S PEANUT BUTTER PIE

2 cups milk
½ cup brown sugar
1 cup white sugar
5 tablespoons corn starch
½ cup evaporated milk
3 egg yolks

⅛ teaspoon salt
¾ cup peanut butter
1 teaspoon vanilla
3 egg whites
¼ teaspoon cream of tartar
2 baked pie shells

Mix milk, brown and white sugar together and bring to boil in heavy
boiler. Mix corn starch, evaporated milk, and egg yolks together. Add to
milk mixture and stir constantly until thick. Add salt and remove from
stove. Beat in peanut butter and vanilla until blended. Beat egg whites
with cream of tartar until stiff and fold in. Pour into baked pie shells. Cool
and cover with whipped topping. Yield: 2 pies.

NANCY'S BUTTERMILK PIE

½ stick melted butter
1 cup sugar
1 tablespoon flour
2 eggs

½ cup buttermilk
½-¾ teaspoon vanilla
9-inch unbaked pie shell

Mix all ingredients together well. Pour into pie shell. Bake in 350° oven
for 30-45 minutes. Yield: 1 pie.

MRS. MASK'S PUMPKIN PIE

1¾ cups cooked pumpkin
2 well-beaten eggs
1 tablespoon pumpkin pie
    spice

⅔ cup sugar
1 teaspoon salt
1½ cups milk
1 unbaked pie shell

Beat eggs well. Add sugar and pumpkin. Sprinkle salt and pumpkin pie spice over mixture. Add milk. Stir all ingredients together well. Pour into unbaked pie shell. Bake in 375° oven for 50 to 55 minutes—or until sharp-bladed knife inserted near center comes out clean. Yield: 1 pie.

VELDA'S GRANDMOTHER'S PUMPKIN PIE

1½-cups cooked pumpkin
¾ cup sugar
½ teaspoon salt
1 teaspoon cinnamon
½ teaspoon ginger
¼ teaspoon nutmeg

¼ teaspoon cloves
3 slightly beaten eggs
1¼ cups milk
1 6-ounce can evaporated milk
1 9-inch unbaked pastry shell

Thoroughly combine pumpkin, sugar, salt and spices. Blend in eggs, milk, and evaporated milk. Pour into unbaked pastry shell—this makes a *big* pie—crimp edges high—filling is generous. Bake at 400° for about 50 minutes. Cool on rack. If baking in glass pie pan, bake for 40 minutes at 400°. Note: We always heat the two milks while we are making the pastry and add the other ingredients to the milk—just heat the milks and that gives the filling a little head-start when pie is put into oven. Yield: 1 large pie.

97

E.J.'S EASY PECAN PIE

2 eggs
1 cup brown sugar
1 cup corn syrup with butter
1 cup pecans

pinch of salt
½ teaspoon vanilla
1 9-inch unbaked pie shell

Beat eggs until light. Add sugar, syrup, salt, pecans and vanilla. Mix well. Pour into unbaked pie shell and bake in 325° oven for 45 minutes or 1 hour until "set". Yield: 1 large pie. 8-10 servings.

MOCK PECAN PIE

1 15-ounce can cooked pinto
  beans
1 small can flaked coconut
3 cups sugar
2 sticks melted margarine
  or butter

4 eggs
1 cup chopped pecans
1 tablespoon vanilla
2 unbaked pie shells

Drain and mash beans real well. In large mixing bowl, beat eggs until slightly thickened. Fold in remaining ingredients and mix well. Pour into pie shells. Bake in preheated 300° oven for 40 minutes. Freezes well for later use. Yield: 2 pies.

RYLE'S BLACKBERRY PIE

6 cups blackberries
1¼ cups sugar
3 tablespoons flour

6 tablespoons butter
1 teaspooon lemon juice
1 9-inch pie crust

Put half of berries in unbaked pie crust. Mix sugar and flour together and put over top of berries. Add remaining berries and dot with butter. Sprinkle lemon juice over pie. Bake in 350° oven for 1 hour. May omit bottom crust and cover top. Slit top crust or make fancy design. Yield: Serves 8.

JANE'S FRESH PEACH COBBLER

2 cups fresh sliced peaches   1 stick butter
1 cup sugar

Mix sugar with peaches and let stand while making batter. Melt butter in 2-quart casserole.

COBBLER BATTER

1 cup sugar
¼ teaspoon salt
1 teaspoon baking powder
¾ cup flour

¾ cup milk
⅛ teaspoon cinnamon
¼ teaspoon almond flavoring

Mix together sugar, salt, baking powder, flour and cinnamon. Beat in milk until no lumps. Pour batter into the melted butter. *Do not stir.* Spoon the peaches over the top of the batter. *Do not stir.* Bake in 350° oven for 45 minutes or until top is golden brown. Yield: Serves 6.

HEMLOCK INN FRUIT COBBLER

4 cups frozen pie cherries
2 cups sugar

3 tablespoons cornstarch
1 stick butter or margarine

Put cherries in 9x13-inch pan. Mix sugar and cornstarch together and sprinkle over cherries. (Leave juice in cherries.) Dot with butter or margarine. Cover with pie pastry. We always use the pastry in the pie section of this book. Bake in 425° oven for approximately 30 minutes or until crust is golden brown. Yield: Serves 18.

You may substitute peaches, blueberries, blackberries or apples. With apples add nutmeg and cinnamon to taste.

Our
   Heavenly
      Father,
we thank Thee
for a good night of rest
   and a new day.
Our prayer is that
we might do what is pleasing to Thee.
We thank Thee for Thy mercy and Thy strength,
   and now for this food.

In Jesus' name we ask it. Amen.

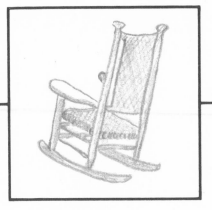

Relishes

MASHBURN'S UNCOOKED RELISH

1 cup bell pepper	2½ tablespoons salt
1 cup red sweet pepper	1 teaspoon celery seed
1 hot pepper	1 pint vinegar
2 cups cabbage	2 cups sugar
½ pound onion	

Chop all vegetables and drain. Add salt. Let stand overnight. Drain again real well. Add celery seed, vinegar and sugar. Store in refrigerator. Serves: 10.

CARROT-CUCUMBER RELISH

3½ cups coarsely ground
   unpeeled cucumbers
1½ cups coarsely ground
   carrots
1 cup coarsely ground medium
   onions

2 tablespoons salt
2½ cups sugar
1½ cups vinegar
1½ teaspoon celery seed
1½ teaspoon mustard seed

Wash and cut off ends of 4 to 6 cucumbers. Peel and cut off ends of 6 medium carrots. Combine ground cucumbers, carrots, onions and salt and let stand 3 hours. Drain well. Combine sugar, vinegar, celery seed and mustard seed and bring to boil. Add vegetables and simmer, uncovered, for 20 minutes. Seal at once in sterilized jars. Yield: 3 pints.

MYRTLE'S SOMETHING GOOD

1 quart chopped apples, peeled
1 quart chopped cabbage
1 quart chopped green tomatoes
1 quart chopped onions
2 tablespoons prepared mustard

1 quart chopped sweet peppers
1 quart vinegar
1 quart sugar
2 tablespoons salt

Use green and red peppers both if you can find sweet peppers like this. Mix really well all ingredients and cook at low boil for 20 minutes. Seal in sterilized jars. Yield: 8 pints.

DADDY'S AND NELL'S PICKLED EGGS

15-18 hard boiled eggs
4 cups vinegar
1 cup water and red food color
**   or 1 cup beet juice**

1 teaspoon salt

Combine vinegar, water, red food color and salt (we use beet juice instead of water and food color) and bring to a boil. Place shelled eggs in a gallon glass jar. Pour hot liquid over eggs. Place in refrigerator overnight or longer. Yield: 15-18.

EASY WATERMELON RIND PICKLES

10 pounds prepared watermelon
**   rind**
12 pounds sugar
1 quart white vinegar

40 drops oil of cloves
40 drops oil of cinnamon
few drops green color

Peel rind and cut into desired pieces. Let stand in cold water for 24 hours. Drain. Cover with fresh water, bring to boil and let simmer 10 minutes. Drain. Dry on tea towel. Weigh. Mix sugar, vinegar, cloves, cinnamon, and green color (we use spinach water or any natural green vegetable juice) together and let stand 24 hours, stirring occasionally. Bring to a boil. Boil 7 to 10 minutes. Pack in sterilized jars and seal. Yield: 8 pints.

CRYSTAL PICKLES

CRYSTAL PICKLES

Relishes*

1 gallon sliced cucumbers	3 pints vinegar
1 cup salt	8 cups sugar
2 teaspoons alum	2 tablespoons pickling spices

Wash and slice cucumbers into container. Pour salt over them and fill with water. Let set 7 days, stirring occasionally.

8th day — Pour water off. Pour boiling water over and let stand overnight.

9th day — Pour water off. Put alum in mixture. Pour boiling water over mixture and let stand overnight.

10th day — Pour water off. Rinse well. Pour boiling water over and let stand overnight.

11th day — Pour water off. Rinse again. Mix vinegar, 6 cups sugar, pickling spices, and pour over mixture. Let set overnight.

12th day — Pour vinegar mixture into pan. Add 1 cup dissolved sugar. Pour over mixture and let set overnight.

13th day — Repeat 12th day.

14th day — Pour vinegar mixture into sauce pan. Boil. Put cucumber mixture into sterilized jars. Pour boiling vinegar mixture over them and seal.

Yield: 6 pints.

BESS PERRY'S PICKLES

4 quarts thinly sliced cucumbers	1½ teaspoon turmeric
6 large onions	2 tablespoons mustard seed
2 green peppers	5 cups sugar
2 pods garlic	2 cups vinegar
1½ teaspoon celery seed	½ cup salt

Slice onions, cucumbers, peppers. Cover with salt and mix all ingredients together. Cover with ice and soak 3 hours. Combine other ingredients and pour over drained cucumbers, onions and peppers. Heat to boiling and seal in sterilized jars. Yield: 6 pints.

105

GRAPE JUICE

Blue concord grapes   **Water**
Sugar

Stem grapes. Wash and put in kettle with barely enough water to cover grapes. Boil until all seeds are free and juice seems to be cooked out. Drain in a bag. (We use clean ham sack.) Return juice to kettle and bring to boil. Add ⅓ *cup sugar to each quart of juice.* Let boil rapidly for 5 minutes. Seal in sterilized jars. (If you plan to make jelly from the juice later, do not add sugar when canning the juice.)

GRAPE JELLY

4 cups grape juice   **3 cups sugar**

Cook grapes according to grape juice recipe. (Leave out sugar.) Pour juice into large crock container and let stand in refrigerator for 24 to 48 hours. Strain again to remove crystals which will be seen clinging to sides of jar. Place juice in large kettle. Boil rapidly for 5 minutes. Add sugar, and boil until it reaches the jelly stage. Pour into hot, sterilized jars and seal. Yield: 3-4 pints.

DAMSON PLUM PRESERVES

1½ quarts damson plums or   5½ cups sugar
  3 pounds ripe plums   1 cup water

Sort and wash plums. Remove pits. Dissolve sugar in water and bring to boil. Add plums and boil, stirring gently, to 221 degrees; or until fruit is transparent and the syrup is thick. Remove preserves from heat and ladle at once into sterlized jars. Seal. Yield: 3 pints.

PEAR JAM

3 pounds ripe soft pears   1 box powdered fruit pectin
4½ cups sugar

Peel and core pears. Grind thoroughly. Measure sugar into a dry dish and set aside until needed. Measure prepared pears into a 5 or 6 quart kettle. Be sure you have 3½ cups of pears. Add water, if necessary, to make the 3½ cups. Add pectin, mix well, and continue stirring until mixture comes to rolling boil. Add sugar and stir constantly. Continue stirring and bring to full rolling boil again. Boil hard for 1 minute. Remove from heat, skim, pour quickly into sterilized jars. Seal. Yield: 3-4 pints.

Our
    Heavenly Father,
we have already felt Thy presence
    this Sunday, and for this
we are so grateful. We thank Thee
for a day that we might wait on Thee
    and we pray that this would be a special day,
        and that Thou would speak to us especially.
We thank Thee for Thy mercy and this lovely day, and
    now for this food.   *In Jesus' name we ask it. Amen.*

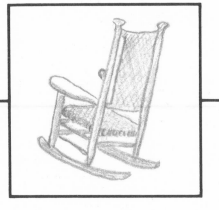

Salads &
Salad
Dressings

RHUBARB-STRAWBERRY SALAD

1 6-ounce package strawberry
  jello
1 cup boiling water
1 10-ounce package frozen
  strawberries

1 10-ounce package frozen
  rhubarb
⅓ cup sugar
pinch of salt

Cook rhubarb as directed on package with sugar. Let cool. Thaw strawberries. Mix jello with boiling water. Add strawberries and rhubarb to jello mixture. Pour into mold and refrigerate until firm. Yield: Serves 12.

JANE'S CHERRY JELLO SALAD

1 1-pound can pie cherries
1 6-ounce package cherry jello
1 tablespoon gelatin
1 tablespoon cold water
1 1-pound can crushed pineapple

1 grated orange peel
1 grated lemon peel
½ cup chopped pecans
pinch of salt
¾ cup granulated sugar

Drain pie cherries real well. Drain real well crushed pineapple. Mix jello with 1 cup boiling water. Add 1 cup *only* of juice from mixture of cherry and pineapple juice. Mix gelatin with cold water and add to hot jello mixture. Grate orange and lemon and add pecans, salt, and sugar. Add to jello mixture and mix all ingredients together. Put in large pyrex dish. Let set in refrigerator until firm. Yield: Serves 12.

APPLESAUCE SALAD

1 1-pound can applesauce
1 8-ounce can crushed pineapple
1 6-ounce package cherry jello

½ cup chopped pecans
pinch of salt

Mix applesauce and cherry jello together in heavy saucepan. Bring to boil. Stir in drained crushed pineapple, salt, and pecans. Put in pyrex dish and refrigerate until firm. Yield: Serves 8.

MIL'S ORANGE-PINEAPPLE SALAD

1 1-pound can crushed pineapple
1 6-ounce package orange jello
2 cups buttermilk

1 8-ounce carton frozen
prepared whipped topping

Mix crushed pineapple and jello together and put in boiler. Bring slowly to boil. Set aside and let cool. Add buttermilk and fold in whipped topping. Yield: Serves 12.

EMERALD SALAD

1 6-ounce package lime jello
¾ cup boiling water
1½ cups grated cucumber and
    rind

1 8-ounce carton cottage cheese
1 cup mayonnaise
2 tablespoons grated onion
¾ cup slivered almonds

Mix real well jello with boiling water. Let cucumbers drain until they don't even drip. Mix cucumbers and onion with jello mixture. Fold in cottage cheese and mayonnaise. Add almonds. Yield: Serves 12.

WALDORF SALAD

1 cup chopped apples
2 tablespoons marashino
  cherries

½ cup chopped English walnuts
½ cup diced celery
½ cup mayonnaise

Mix fruit, walnuts, celery and mayonnaise. Chill and serve immediately. Yield: Serves 4.

APPLE-RAISIN SALAD

4 Red Delicious apples
½ cup plumped raisins
2 tablespoons mayonnaise

2 teaspoons lemon juice
pinch of salt

To plump raisins, soak in water for about 10 minutes. Drain well. Core and cut apples into bite sizes. Do not peel. Mix with raisins and toss with mayonnaise and lemon juice. Sprinkle with salt. Serve immediately. Yield: Serves 10.

JACKIE'S FRUIT SALAD

1 1-pound can fruit cocktail
¼ head lettuce
1 banana

1 tablespoon powdered sugar
1 teaspoon mayonnaise

Drain fruit cocktail real well. Break up lettuce into bite sizes. Cut banana into slices. Toss with mayonnaise and sugar. Serve immediately. Yield: Serves 4.

LOUISE'S LUNCHEON SALAD

1 10½-ounce can condensed
    tomato soup
1½ tablespoons unflavored
    gelatin
½ cup cold water
2 3-ounce packages cream
    cheese

1 cup chopped celery
2 tablespoons chopped green
    pepper
1 teaspoon minced onion
½ cup sliced olives
½ cup broken English walnuts
1 cup mayonnaise

Heat tomato soup; add gelatin softened in cold water. Cool. Thoroughly combine remaining ingredients. Add to gelatin mixture. Pour into mold. Chill until firm. Yield: Serves 8.

HON'S TART ASPARAGUS SALAD

2 envelopes unflavored gelatin
½ cup cold water
¾ cup sugar
½ cup vinegar
1 cup water
1 tablespoon minced onion
2 tablespoons lemon juice

1 10-ounce can cut green
    asparagus
1 cup chopped pimentos
1 teaspoon salt
1 5-ounce can water chestnuts
1 cup chopped celery

Mix gelatin and cold water together. Bring sugar, vinegar and 1 cup water to boil. Add to gelatin mixture. Add onion and lemon juice. Allow to cool. Add sliced water chestnuts and chopped celery. Let jell. Yield: Serves 8.

BEULAH'S KRAUT SALAD

1 1-pound can shredded kraut
⅓ cup oil
½ cup sugar
1 cup sliced onion

1 cup chopped celery
1 cup chopped bell pepper
1 3-ounce can pimentos

Drain kraut real well. Mix together oil, sugar and add to kraut. Mix onion, celery, bell pepper and pimentos and add to kraut mixture. Let stand at least 6 hours before serving. Yield: Serves 12.

LYDAY'S CALICO SALAD

1 1-pound can cut green beans
1 1-pound can cut wax beans
1 1-pound can kidney beans
½ cup chopped bell pepper
½ cup chopped red sweet onion

¾ cup sugar
⅔ cup vinegar
⅓ cup oil
1 teaspoon salt
¾ teaspoon pepper

Drain beans and mix together. Add chopped onion and pepper. Combine sugar, vinegar, oil, salt, and pepper and add to bean mixture. Refrigerate overnight. Take out of refrigerator 1 hour before serving. Yield: Serves 12.

Salads

DODY'S APRICOT-CHEESE DELIGHT

1 20-ounce can drained crushed pineapple
1 20-ounce can drained and cut apricots
1 cup marshmallows

2 cups juice from pineapple and apricots
2 3-ounce packages orange jello
2 cups boiling water

Drain pineapple and apricots. Mix jello with boiling water and add 1 cup juice. Add marshmallows and stir until they are melted. When this mixture starts to jell, add pineapple and apricots. Put topping on:

½ cup sugar
3 tablespoons flour
1 beaten egg
¼ teaspoon salt

2 cups grated cheddar cheese
1 cup whipping cream
2 tablespoons butter

Mix well the first 5 ingredients and add the remaining cup of juice. Cook over low heat until thick. Remove from heat and add butter. Cool thoroughly. Fold in whipping cream. After fruit mixture is congealed, spread this evenly over it and sprinkle with cheese. Refrigerate for 24 hours before serving. Yield: Serves 18.

DODY'S 24-HOUR SALAD

2 1-pound 4-ounce cans crushed and drained pineapple
1 pound miniature marshmallows
½ cup pecans
1 10-ounce bottle of drained maraschino cherries

1 quart whipping cream
4 eggs
3 tablespoons sugar
½ teaspoon salt
¾ cup milk
1 tablespoon flour
3 tablespoons vinegar

Mix pineapple, marshmallows, pecans and cherries after chopping into pieces. Whip cream and fold into fruit mixture. Pour into 9x13-inch pan. To make topping, mix sugar, salt, flour and vinegar together. Beat eggs and add milk. Combine topping ingredients and cook slowly until mixture begins to thicken. When cold, pour over salad. Put in refrigerator for 24 hours. Yield: Serves 20.

115

LOIS' FRUIT SALAD

½ cup sugar
1 3-ounce cream cheese
1 22-ounce can cherry pie filling
1 1-pound 4-ounce can pineapple
   chunks

1 cup pecans
½ pint whipping cream

Cream together cream cheese and sugar. Add pie filling (may substitute blueberry or strawberry filling), pineapple and pecans. Whip cream and fold into mixture. Put in bake-cups in muffin pans until frozen. Remove from muffin pans and place in airtight container and keep in freezer. Will keep for several weeks. Yield: Serves 12.

MARY ANN'S CHRISTMAS SALAD

1 16-ounce box cranberries
2 oranges
2 cups sugar

2 3-ounce packages raspberry
   jello
¾ cup pecans

Grind cranberries and oranges together (include rind of oranges). Sprinkle sugar over mixture and let set. Mix jello with 1 *only* cup boiling water. Leave juice of cranberries and oranges and mix all together. Add pecans. Yield: Serves 12.

HEMLOCK INN SALAD DRESSING

1 teaspoon salt	½ teaspoon basil
6 tablespoons sugar	½ teaspoon parsley flakes
1 teaspoon garlic powder	½ cup vinegar
½ teaspoon oregano	1½ cups mayonnaise

Mix all ingredients together real well. Yield: Approximately 2½ cups.

May add ketchup for French dressing.

WARREN'S BLUE CHEESE DRESSING

1 16-ounce carton sour cream	2 large cloves of garlic
2 8-ounce packages of blue cheese	1 teaspoon vinegar
2 tablespoons of peanut oil	pinch of salt and pepper

Put sour cream in medium-sized mixing bowl. Use garlic press and put crushed garlic and juice in sour cream mixture. Break blue cheese into small bits and add. Fold in oil and vinegar until smooth. Add salt and pepper to taste. Yield: 24 servings.

SYLVIA'S SWEET DRESSING

1 teaspoon celery seed	1 teaspoon grated onion
1 teaspoon dry mustard	½ cup honey
1 teaspoon salt	1 cup vegetable oil
1 teaspoon paprika	¼ cup tarragon vinegar

Mix all ingredients together well. Serve over fresh fruit in season. Especially good over fresh grapefruit and avocado. Yield: 1 pint.

Our Heavenly Father,
    how happy we are
to pause and give Thee thanks
for this lovely day and for Thy love.
We are so grateful that Thou dost care for us
    and watch over us, and particularly that thou dost
call us by our first name. Thank you for these good friends ·
and now for this food.   *In Jesus' name we ask it. Amen.*

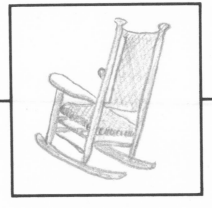

Soups
& Sauces

FAVORITE WHITE SAUCE

1 tablespoon butter   pinch of salt
1 tablespoon flour   1 cup milk

In heavy saucepan, melt butter. Stir in flour, and slowly add milk. Stir constantly with whisk until thick. Yield: 1 cup.

BARBECUE SAUCE

¼ cup butter or margarine   ½ cup peanut oil
½ cup vinegar   2 tablespoons catsup
1 crushed garlic clove   1½ tablespoons Worcestershire
⅓ cup lemon juice   sauce
1 teaspoon lemon rind grated   1 tablespoon salt
½ teaspoon red pepper   ½ teaspoon pepper

Mix all ingredients together well. Bring mixture to boil. Remove from heat and simmer for 45 minutes. Yield: Serves 10.

VEGETABLE SOUP

leftover beef or chicken
   in its broth
onions
grated carrots

rice
leftover vegetables of any kind
2 cups tomatoes

Our vegetable soup is made from all leftovers. Always we have chopped onions, grated carrots, rice and cooked tomatoes and then anything else we've had during the week. Usually, we add corn, limas, okra, celery, green beans, parsley; but don't go out and buy something for your soup. The more you can use what you have, the better your soup. Salt and pepper to taste. Most of the time your meat and/or vegetables are already seasoned so be careful that you don't add too much. Let cook for about 2 hours. Yield: Serves 12-40.

BEAN SOUP

1 country ham bone
3 medium onions
2 carrots

1 1-pound package great
   northern beans

Put ham bone in heavy boiler with 2 quarts water. Let cook until ham falls off bone (about 1 hour). Remove ham bone and set broth aside. Put beans in a boiler and bring to boil. Set aside in its juice for about 2-3 hours. Chop onions and shred carrots. Add ham broth to bean mixture. Add onions and carrots and bring to boil. Cook slowly for about 2 hours. Yield: Serves 12-40.

Our
    Heavenly Father,
we are blessed
because we know Thee.
We lift our hearts to Thee
    in praise,
and give thanks for this good day,
for Thy mercy, and especially for these friends,
and now for this food.   In Jesus' name we pray. Amen.

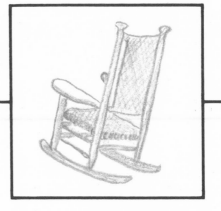

Vegetables

CURRIED FRUIT

½ cup butter
2 cups peach halves
2 cups pear halves
2 cups pineapple tidbits

2 cups apricot halves
½ cup brown sugar
2 teaspoons curry powder

In buttered casserole, place brown sugar and curry powder. Arrange fruit on top of mixture. Bake in 350⁰ oven for 45 minutes to 1 hour. Yield: Serves 12.

DORIS' SHERRIED FRUIT

1 1-pound can sliced pineapple
1 1-pound can peach halves
1 1-pound can pears
1 1-pound can apricot halves
1 1-pound jar apple rings

2 tablespoons flour
1½ cups sugar
1 stick butter
1 cup sherry

Drain all fruits. Cut pineapple and peaches in half and arrange fruit in layers in large, medium shallow, casserole. In double boiler, heat butter, sugar, flour, and sherry over boiling water. Stir constantly until about as thick as cream. Pour over fruit and let stand in refrigerator overnight. Bake in 350⁰ oven about 20 minutes or until thoroughly heated and bubbly. Especially good with roast loin of pork, ham, or poultry. Yield: Serves 12.

RHUBARB

4 cups cut rhubarb pinch of salt
½-1 cup sugar

Wash and trim off ends of rhubarb. Peel like celery. Cut into bite-size pieces and place into small blue roaster. Sprinkle salt and sugar over top. Place in 350⁰ oven and bake for about 1 hour or until well done. Some people like rhubarb to be consistency of applesauce—others like it not so well done. There are many varieties of rhubarb: strawberry, apple, plain (very sour), cherry, and probably several others. It's fun to see different varieties growing—each has it's own color. Yield: Serves 8-10.

E.J.'S CRANBERRIES

2 pounds cranberries 4 cups fresh or frozen diluted
2 cups English walnuts   orange juice
2 cups sugar

Bring sugar and orange juice to boil. Add cranberries and cook 6 minutes. Take off heat, add walnuts, and let cool. Yield: Serves 12.

BAKED APPLES

6 baking apples 2 teaspoons cinnamon
½ cup sugar ¼ cup melted margarine

Wash, core and quarter apples. Leave peelings on apples. Mix sugar and cinnamon together. Place apples in deep baking pan and sprinkle sugar mixture over them. Pour margarine on top. Cover. Bake in 400⁰ oven for about 1 hour. Yield: Serves 8.

Any good baking apple will do. We use Wolf River or Pippin when we can get them. However, the season for these two apples is short; and we use any firm, good apple that we can get during the year.

HARIETT'S SCALLOPED PINEAPPLE

1 cup sugar	½ cup milk
½ cup butter	½ cup pineapple juice
1 1-pound can chunk pineapple	10 slices fresh white bread
2 eggs	cubed

Mix all ingredients together and bake in long greased pan in 375° oven for 30-40 minutes. Yield: Serves 10.

APPLE AND CARROT CASSEROLE

3 cups cooked apples	½ cup sugar
1 cup cooked carrots	½ stick butter or margarine

Slice carrots, cook and drain. Add apples, sugar and melted butter or margarine. Cover and bake in 350° oven for 20 minutes. Yield: Serves 8.

VELDA'S CARROT-PINEAPPLE POSH

3 cups round cut carrots	1 cup white raisins
1 teaspoon salt	½ cup firmly packed light
1 20-ounce can crushed	brown sugar
pineapple with juice	juice of ½ lemon

Cook carrots in salted water until *slightly* tender. Combine carrots with other ingredients in a well-buttered 1½ quart casserole dish. Bake in 350° oven for one hour. Yield: Serves 8.

VELDA'S CARROT CUSTARD

2 cups carrots	½ teaspoon salt
2 eggs	4 tablespoons melted butter or
1 cup bread crumbs	margarine
1½ cups milk	1 teaspoon sugar
1 cup sharp cheese	paprika

Cook and mash carrots. Beat eggs and mix together with milk, salt, butter or margarine and sugar. Grate cheese and add to other ingredients. Place in greased 1½-quart casserole and bake for about 30 minutes in 350° oven. Yield: Serves 10.

PEG'S CARROTS

2 pounds carrots	½ cup vinegar
1 medium red onion	½ cup brown sugar
1 can tomato soup	1 teaspoon dry mustard
½ cup vegetable oil	pinch of salt
2 teaspoons Worcestershire	pinch of pepper
sauce	pinch of garlic powder

Slice and cook carrots until tender; drain and cool. Slice onion. Mix together tomato soup, vegetable oil, vinegar, brown sugar, dry mustard, salt, pepper, and garlic. Simmer for 12 minutes. Add Worcestershire sauce and let cool. Make alternate layers of carrots and onion rings and pour sauce over them. Refrigerate and let stand several hours. Will keep 2 weeks in refrigerator. May be served cold or hot. If served cold, let stand at room temperature for 1 hour before serving. Yield: Serves 10.

Our Father,
　we come to Thee
with grateful hearts for a good day
and Thy mercy.
We especially thank you for the rain. As this rain
refreshes the earth, we pray that Thy Holy Spirit will
　refresh our spirit.
Thank you for loving us and for providing this food.
　　　　　　　　　　　In Jesus' name we ask it. Amen.

OKRA FRITTERS

1 cup self-rising cornmeal
1 10-ounce package frozen okra

peanut oil for deep frying

Combine cornmeal and sufficient water to form a thick batter. Cut frozen okra in small bite-size pieces. Drop by spoonful into hot oil and deep fry until golden brown. Drain on rack and serve hot. Yield: 16

CORN FRITTERS

1¾ cups self-rising flour
pinch of salt
1 teaspoon sugar
2 beaten eggs

½ cup milk
2 tablespoons melted margarine
1 1-pound can whole kernel corn
oil for deep frying

Sift together flour, salt and sugar. Beat eggs well and add milk and melted margarine. Drain corn well and add to other ingredients. Drop by teaspoonfuls into hot oil and deep fry until golden brown. Drain on rack and serve hot. Yield: 24.

Corn can be substituted with bananas, chopped apples, or pineapple.

APPLE FRITTERS

6 Red Delicious apples
1 cup self-rising flour
1 tablespoon sugar

water to make thin batter
oil for deep frying

Wash and core apples and slice into ¼ inch pieces. Mix flour, sugar, and water together. Dip into thin batter and drop into hot oil and deep fat until golden brown. Drain and slightly sprinkle with granulated sugar. Yield: 24.

FRIED ONION RINGS

2 Bermuda onions   ½ cup water
½ cup flour   ½ teaspoon salt

Slice onions into ¼ inch pieces. Mix flour, salt and water together to make batter. Dip onion rings into batter and fry in deep fat (350⁰) for 1-2 minutes or until golden. Drain on paper towel and serve while hot. Yield: Serves 6.

DOT'S VIDALIA ONION PIE

10-12 soda crackers   1 cup white sauce
1 pound Vidalia onions   ¼ pound sharp cheese
⅓ stick margarine

Melt margarine and pour half into the crushed crackers. Blend well. Save enough cracker crumbs to sprinkle over top. Press cracker crumbs into pie pan. Slice the onions thin and saute in remaining margarine until tender but not brown. Put onions on the pie crust and pour over white sauce to which the sharp cheese has been added and melted. Sprinkle a few cracker crumbs over top and bake in 350⁰ oven for about 15 minutes. Yield: Serves 8.

Note: For those of you who don't know about Vidalia onions, let me tell you a little about them. There's a small town in southeast Georgia named Vidalia. The farmers in that area produce an onion that is not only big, healthy, and juicy; but delicious in taste. The citizens of Vidalia attribute the success of this onion to the local soil. No place else in the world, so they say, will this onion grow! And I agree—it is delicious. The season for it is so short—usually just June—so those of us who have learned to love them, rush out to a nearby Georgia fruit stand that gets a few sacks each year!

MAY'S CASSEROLE

6 slices white bread	1 tablespoon chopped onion
2 cups tomatoes	1¼ cups milk
½ teaspoon salt	3 eggs
¼ teaspoon pepper	1 cup grated sharp cheese

Line bottom of buttered casserole with bread slices. Spread drained tomatoes over bread. Add salt, pepper, and finely chopped onion over top of bread and tomatoes. Beat eggs well and add milk. Pour over bread and tomato mixture. Add grated sharp cheese to top. Bake in 350° oven for 1 hour. Yield: Serves 10.

HERBED TOMATOES

4 cups cooked tomatoes	⅛ teaspoon pepper
½ teaspoon basil	⅛ teaspoon allspice
½ teaspoon oregano	⅛ teaspoon cloves
¼ cup brown sugar	10-12 soda crackers
1 teaspoon salt	

Mix together tomatoes, basil, oregano, brown sugar, salt, pepper, allspice, and cloves. Simmer 45 minutes. Break up crackers in serving dish, and pour tomato mixture over them. Yield: Serves 10.

Vegetables

HARVARD BEETS

2½ cups sliced beets
⅔ cup sugar
4 teaspoons cornstarch

½ cup vinegar
½ cup beet liquid
2 tablespoons margarine

Combine sugar and cornstarch. Stir into vinegar and beet liquid. Stir over low heat until thickened. Add beets and margarine. Heat slowly. Yield: Serves 10.

VELDA'S FRENCH BEETS

2 teaspoons minced onion
2 teaspoons chopped green
   pepper
2 teaspoons dry parsley

1 teaspoon lemon juice or
   vinegar
1 can French style julienne
   beets

Mix all ingredients together, heat and serve. Yield: Serves 4.

ASPARAGUS CASSEROLE

1 tablespoon butter
¼ cup grated sharp cheese
3 hard-boiled eggs
1 can asparagus soup
1 1-pound can cut asparagus
2 eggs

½ cup powdered milk
juice of lemon
½ teaspoon salt
¼ teaspoon pepper
½ onion powder
½ cup bread crumbs

Mix soup, eggs, powdered milk, lemon juice, salt, pepper, and onion powder together. Chop the hard-boiled eggs and add half of bread crumbs. Add to soup mixture. In casserole pour soup mixture and put asparagus on top. Sprinkle grated cheese on top and add remaining bread crumbs. Dot with butter. Bake in 350° oven until brown about 20 minutes. Yield: Serves 8.

FROSTED CAULIFLOWER

1 head cauliflower
½ cup mayonnaise

2 teaspoons prepared mustard
¾ cup shredded sharp cheese

Cook cauliflower, leaving whole. Drain and place whole cauliflower in shallow casserole. Frost wiht mayonnaise mixed with mustard. Sprinkle with cheese. Bake in 350° oven until cheese melts, about 10 minutes. Yield: Serves 8.

VELDA'S ORIENTAL CABBAGE

½ cup melted margarine
1 medium head chopped
  cabbage
1 green pepper
2 stalks celery
2 carrots

1 large onion
¾ cup evaporated milk
dash of salt
dash of pepper
1 scant teaspoon sugar

Cut green pepper into strips. Chop celery and carrots thin and slanted. Slice onion into rings. Melt margarine and add vegetables in a large skillet. Cover and cook over medium heat for 10 minutes. Stir in milk and heat thoroughly. Add salt, pepper and sugar to taste. Yield: Serves 8.

IRMA'S BROCCOLI CASSEROLE

2 cups cooked broccoli
½ cup thick white sauce
½ cup mayonnaise
2 teaspoons onion juice

3 eggs well beaten
dash of salt
dash of pepper

Combine all ingredients and pour into well-greased 1 quart casserole. Set in pan of hot water and bake in 350⁰ oven for about 45 minutes.

WHITE SAUCE

1½ tablespoons flour
1½ tablespoons butter or
    margarine

½ cup milk

Yield: Serves 10.

FAVORITE BROCCOLI CASSEROLE

2 packages frozen chopped
    broccoli
1 can cream of mushroom soup
2 tablespoons grated onion

2 well-beaten eggs
1 cup sharp grated cheese
1 cup mayonnaise
buttered bread crumbs

Cook broccoli until tender and drain. Mix soup, onion, eggs, cheese and mayonnaise and fold in thoroughly. Layer broccoli and sauce in greased casserole. Add buttered bread crumbs. Bake in 350⁰ oven for 20 to 30 minutes. Yield: Serves 8.

GREEN RICE

1½ cups cooked rice
2 tablespoons ground onion
½ pound package chopped
    frozen spinach
¼ teaspoon garlic salt

¼ pound margarine
1¼ cups sharp cheese
2 eggs
2 cups milk
1 teaspoon salt

Mix rice, onion, spinach, garlic salt, margarine, milk, and salt together. Grate cheese. Beat eggs thoroughly. Add cheese and eggs to other ingredients. Put into large casserole and bake for 1 hour in 300° oven. Yield: Serves 12.

WILTED LETTUCE

½ head lettuce
2 fresh Spring onions
1 tablespoon bacon drippings

1 tablespoon water
1 tablespoon real bacon bits
salt to taste

Cut up lettuce and onions together and place in serving bowl. Heat bacon drippings to *hot* temperature. Pour over lettuce and onion mixture. Pour water into hot skillet and immediately pour over lettuce. Sprinkle salt on top and toss in bacon bits. Yield: Serves 8.

CORN PUDDING

3 cups corn
1½ cups warm milk
2 tablespoons margarine
½ teaspoon salt

dash of pepper
1 tablespoon sugar
3 tablespoons flour
4 eggs

Beat eggs thoroughly. Add sugar and flour together and add to egg mixture. Mix corn, margarine, salt, pepper, and warm milk together. Add to egg mixture. Pour into greased 1½-quart casserole. Bake in 300° oven for about 45 minutes. Yield: Serves 10.

VELDA'S EGGPLANT CASSEROLE

1 medium eggplant
1 small onion
1 cup milk
2 eggs
½ cup bread crumbs

dash of salt
dash of pepper
1 tablespoon sugar
4 tablespoons butter or
   margarine

Peel, cut in chunks, and boil until tender the eggplant. Drain well and mash. Add salt, pepper and sugar. Chop finely onion and add to mixture. Beat eggs well and add milk. Add to other ingredients. Top with butter or margarine that has been melted and mixed with the bread crumbs. Bake in 400° oven for 25 minutes. Yield: Serves 8.

SWEET POTATO CASSEROLE

3 cups cooked mashed sweet
    potatoes
½ cup sugar
½ teaspoon salt

½ stick margarine
½ cup milk
1½ teaspoons vanilla
2 eggs

Mix sweet potatoes, sugar, salt, margarine, milk, vanilla, and eggs.
Spoon into baking dish. Use topping if desired.

TOPPING

½ cup brown sugar
⅓ cup flour

1 cup chopped pecans
⅓ stick margarine

Mix and crumble over potatoes. Bake in 350° oven for 35 minutes. Yield:
Serves 10.

OKRA, TOMATOES AND ONIONS

3 cups cook tomatoes
1 10-ounce package frozen cut
    okra

1 large onion

Thaw okra. Slice onion in rings. Mix okra, onion slices and tomatoes
together. Cook slowly in heavy boiler for about 30 minutes or until onions
and okra are thoroughly cooked. Yield: Serves 8.

AUNT HATTIE'S SQUASH SOUFFLE

1 quart cooked and drained
   squash
1 cup bread crumbs
½ cup dry milk
1 pint squash broth
2 tablespoons ground onion
1 tablespoon ground green
   pepper

2 eggs
2 tablespoons sugar
1 teaspoon salt
2 tablespoons melted margarine
½ teaspoon accent

Soak milk, crumbs and broth for 15 minutes. Add to squash. Add onion and green pepper to mixture. Beat eggs well and add to squash mixture. Add sugar, salt, margarine and add accent to ingredients and pour into greased casserole. Bake in 300º oven for 35 minutes. Yield: Serves 10.

HEMLOCK TRAIN WRECK

½ teaspoon pepper
1 teaspoon salt
1 pound zucchini
⅓ cup real bacon bits

2 large onions
½ cup catsup
1 tablespoon dried basil

Wash, but do not peel zucchini. Cut into slices. Slice onions and separate into rings. Slightly brown onions. In casserole place layer of zucchini slices, sprinkle with salt, pepper, dried basil, and dot with catsup. Cover with layer of onions and bacon bits. Repeat until casserole is filled. Cover and cook in 350º oven for 1½ hours. Yield: Serves 10.

CANDY ROASTER

candy roaster
brown sugar
cinnamon

melted butter or margarine
slightly salted boiling water

The first time I heard "candy roaster" shortly after we moved to these mountains, I thought it was the name of a black pot with legs. When our cook stopped laughing, she told me that that pot was a "spider-pot" and a "candy roaster" was a bright orange (usually) fall squash. (I still have a hard time recognizing a *good* candy roaster; but I am better.) Nothing is better in the fall to serve with country ham and baked apples.

Wash the candy roaster with a pot scrubber. Cut, take out seeds and pulp and cut into 3-inch squares. Drop into boiling water for about 3 to 5 minutes (or until fork barely sticks in pulp). Take out, drain real well and place onto baking pan. Make thick paste of brown sugar, pinch of cinnamon (to taste) and melted butter or margarine. Ice candy roaster with topping and bake in 375° oven for about 20 minutes or until topping bubbles. (Be careful not to cook too long as brown sugar is easily scorched —remember!) Yield: Serves 100!

For a family, buy smallest candy roaster available and freeze after boiling stage. Take out whenever you want.

½ cup brown sugar
¼ cup melted butter or
   margarine

¼ teaspoon cinnamon

This amount ices approximately 12 pieces of 3-inch squares of candy roaster.

MENU SAMPLE

BREAKFAST

Orange Juice		Hot Apple Sauce
Bacon	or	Country Ham
Poached Eggs		Scrambled Eggs
Country Milled Grits		Country Milled Grits

Coffee/Tea/Sanka/Hot Chocolate/Milk
Home-made Biscuits
Jellies/Jams

Lunch is never served at Hemlock Inn except on Sunday.

BOX LUNCH

Pimento cheese sandwich
Ham biscuits
Hard boiled egg
Apple
Home-made cookies

DINNER

*Country Fried Steak/Baked Potatoes
Chicken/Dumplings*

*Green Beans
Aunt Hattie's Squash Souffle
Okra/Tomatoes/Onions
Apples/Carrots*

Old Fashioned Lemon Pie

*Home-made Rolls
Apple/Pumpkin Chips
Something Good (Relish)*

Iced Tea/Hot tea/Coffee/Milk/Sanka

*Breakfasts and dinners are different each day.
This is just a sample.*

Our Father, for these friends that sustain us socially;
for this food that sustains us physically;
and for Thy saving Grace that does sustain us spiritually;
We give Thee thanks. Amen.

List of Photographs

1. Sign at entrance on Galbraith Creek Road.
2. Lamp post with flag at beginning of walk.
3. Hanging basket at end of first building.
4. Wormy chestnut cupboards in dining room - gifts for sale.
5. Hemlock Inn main building with hemlock in foreground.
6. Steps at unit number six.
7. Swain County Court House. Bryson City is the county seat.
8. Lazy Susan table in dining room.
9. Old pot, gun and dulcimer.
10. Fireplace in dining room.
11. Cozy reading corner near fireplace.
12. Morning paper from sunroom window.
13. Deacon's bench at breezeway unit number seven.
14. Thomas Chapel, Galbraith Creek Road. Originally built in 1860. The people of the community cut the timber and brought the logs in with a team of oxen.
15. Table-setting at Hemlock Inn.
16. Tom's Branch Falls in Deep Creek inside the Great Smoky Mountains National Park, three miles from Hemlock Inn. A favorite hiking place for our guests - two miles of easy walking, tubing or picnicking.
17. Rocking chair with flowers on a misty morning at the Hemlock Inn.
18. Old lantern at walkway.
19. Farmstead at Oconoluftee Visitor's Center on road to Gatlinburg, four miles from Cherokee. A typical farm in the Smokies in the early 1800's.
20. Front porch in autumn with pumpkins.

Lord,
    Our plates are full;
    Our friends are near;
    Our hearts are warm;
    Our thanks sincere.
                Amen.

WEIGHTS AND MEASURES

English:

1 tablespoon = 3 teaspoons
¼ cup = 4 tablespoons = 2 fluid ounces
⅓ cup = 5⅓ tablespoons
½ cup = 8 tablespoons = 4 fluid ounces
1 cup = 16 tablespoons = 8 fluid ounces
2 cups = 1 pint = 16 fluid ounces
4 cups = 1 quart = 32 fluid ounces
4 quarts = 1 gallon
8 quarts = 1 peck
4 pecks = 1 bushel
1 pound = 16 ounces

Abbreviations:
  cm = centimeter
  g = gram
  kg = kilogram
  ml = milliliter

Metric:

Liquid or Dry Measures:
¼ cup = 59 ml
⅓ cup = 79 ml
½ cup = 118 ml
⅔ cup = 152 ml
¾ cup = 176 ml
1 cup = 237 ml
2 cups = 473 ml
4 cups = 946 ml

Dry Measures:
1 tablespoon = 14.9 ml
1 teaspoon = 4.9 ml
½ teaspoon = 2.5 ml
¼ teaspoon = 1.2 ml

Weights:
The actual weight of an ounce = 28.35g (grams).

Weights:	Grams:
½ oz.	= 14 g
1 oz.	= 28 g
2 oz.	= 57 g
3 oz	= 85 g
4 oz.	= 113 g
5 oz.	= 142 g
6 oz.	= 170 g
8 oz.	= 227 g
10 oz.	= 284 g
12 oz.	= 340 g
1 lb.	= 454 g
2½ lb.	= 0.91kg
3 lb.	= 1.35kg

Volume Measures:
1 gallon = 3.79 liters
1 quart = .95 liters
1 pint = .48 liters

Our Heavenly Father,
  how glad we are to come
to Thee as this day closes
  and we come
with Thanksgiving in our hearts.
We thank you for this lovely day, and for
  Thy mercy and continued watchcare. We thank you
for good friends and answered prayers, and especially now
for this food.   *In Jesus' name we ask it. Amen.*

TABLE OF EQUIVALENTS

FOOD EQUIVALENTS

Apples	3 pounds	= about 2 quarts, sliced
Baking Powder	1 t. single-acting	= ¾ t. double-acting
Cheese	1 pound	= 4½ cups
Cottage Cheese	1 pound	= 2 cups
Chocolate, unsweetened	1 square (1 oz.)	= 3-4 T. grated chocolate
Cornstarch	1 T.	= 2 T. flour
Crackers, graham	3 cups crumbs	= 30-36 crackers
Crackers, salted	1 cup fine crumbs	= 20 crackers
Dates, pitted	1 pound	= 2 cups
Eggs		
Whole	1 egg	= about 3 T.
	1 cup	= 5-6 eggs
Whites	1 white	= about 2 T.
	1 cup	= 8-10 whites
Yolks	1 yolk	= about 1 T.
	1 cup	= 14-16 yolks
Figs, chopped	1 pound	= 3 cups
Flour, unsifted	1 pound	= 3 cups
All-purpose, sifted once	1 pound	= 3¾ cups
Cake, sifted once	1 pound	= 2 cups
Gelatin, unflavored	1 envelope (Knox)	= 1 T.
Lemon	1 average size	= 2-3 T. juice, 3 T. rind
Lentils	1 cup dry	= 2 cups cooked
Macaroni	1-1¼ cups dry (4 oz.)	= 2¼ cups cooked
Marshmallows	½ pound	= 30 standard size
	1 standard size	= 10 miniature
Noodles	1½-2 cups dry (4 oz.)	= 2¼ cups cooked
Prunes, dried	1 pound, dried	= 2½ cups
	1 pound, cooked	= 4 cups
Punch	1 gallon	= serves approx. 20
	12 quarts	= 96 punch glasses
Raisins	1 pound seeded	= 2½ cups
	1 pound seedless	= 3 cups
Rice	1 cup raw	= 3-3½ cups cooked
	1 cup pre-cooked	= 2 cups
Shortening, Butter	1 pound	= 2 cups
	½ pound	= 2 sticks
	1 stick	= ½ cup or 8 T.
Spaghetti	1-1¼ cup raw (4 oz.)	= 2½ cups cooked
Sugar		
Brown, sieved and packed	1 pound	= 2⅛ cups
Confectioners' sifted	1 pound	= about 4 cups
Granulated	1 pound	= 2⅛ cups
Yeast	1 cake yeast	= 1 level T. active dry
	1 pkg. dry yeast	= 1 level T. active dry
Vanilla Wafers	1 cup crumbs	= about 22 wafers
Zwieback	1 cup crumbs	= 8-9 slices

JUDY'S BLUEBERRY DELIGHT

1¼ cups graham cracker
  crumbs
¼ cup sugar
¼ cup softened butter
3 bananas
1 quart fresh blueberries

1 8-ounce package cream
  cheese
1 cup sugar
1 9-ounce package prepared
  whipped topping

Blend graham cracker crumbs well with fork and add sugar and softened butter. Press mixture firmly inside well-buttered 9x13-inch pyrex dish. Bake in 375° oven for 8 minutes. Let cool. Cream together cream cheese, 1 cup sugar and mix thoroughly. Slice bananas and place on top of crust. Add alternately whipped topping and blueberries until dish is full. Let set for 2 hours in refrigerator. Yield: Serves 12.

BANANA SPLIT CAKE

1 stick margarine
2 cups graham cracker crumbs
1 8-ounce package cream
  cheese
1 cup sugar
1 9-ounce package prepared
  whipped topping

4 or 5 bananas
1 20-ounce can crushed
  pineapple, drained well
Maraschino cherries
chopped nuts

Melt 1 stick margarine. Stir 2 cups graham cracker crumbs into melted margarine and pack in 11x13-inch pan. Blend together cream cheese, sugar and whipped topping. Slice bananas over crust. Drain pineapple (should drain about 2 hours). Put layers of cheese mix and bananas and pineapple. Put cherries and nuts on top layer. Chill until firm. Yield: Serves 12.

HEMLOCK BRAN MUFFINS

3 cups white sugar
5 cups flour
1 15-ounce package raisin bran
1 teaspoon salt
5 teaspoons baking soda

4 eggs (slightly beaten)
1 quart buttermilk
2 sticks melted butter or
  margarine

Mix dry ingredients together in a large bowl. Mix wet ingredients together and fold into the dry. Place in covered bowl in refrigerator and take out desired amount as needed. Batter will keep for two months.

CRUNCHY CAULIFLOWER SALAD

1 medium head cauliflower
1 cup sliced radishes
½ cup sliced green onion
1 8-ounce can sliced water
    chestnuts, drained
¾ cup commercial sour cream

¾ cup mayonnaise
2 tablespoons caraway seeds
1 (0.37 ounce) package
    buttermilk salad dressing
    mix

Wash the cauliflower, and break into flowerets. Combine cauliflower and next 3 ingredients in a medium bowl, toss gently. Stir together remaining ingredients. Pour over vegetables and stir well. Spoon into serving bowl. Cover and chill before serving. Yield: Serves 8.

HEMLOCK INN BISCUITS

6 cups self-rising flour
3 tablespoons baking powder

1½ cups pure lard (or Crisco)
2-2¼ cups buttermilk

Sift flour and baking powder together into bowl. Cut in lard until mixture is like coarse crumbs. Blend in just enough buttermilk with fork until dough leaves sides of bowl (too much makes dough too sticky to handle, not enough makes biscuits dry). Knead gently 10-12 strokes on a lightly floured surface. Split dough in half, rolling each half until about ½-inch thick. Cut out biscuits without twisting cutter and brush buttermilk on tops. Bake at 500° until golden brown — approximately 8-10 minutes. Yield: 8 dozen small biscuits.

SPINACH-ARTICHOKE CASSEROLE

2 10-ounce packages frozen
    spinach
1 package frozen artichokes
    (or 12¾-ounce can)
½ cup butter or margarine
bread crumbs

1 8-ounce package cream
    cheese
1 teaspoon lemon juice
salt and pepper to taste
Lea and Perrin's sauce to taste

Cook frozen vegetables according to directions on packages. Drain spinach and put cream cheese and butter in pan so that it will melt into spinach. Put artichokes on bottom of buttered casserole or individual ramekins. Add lemon juice to spinach mixture and put over artichokes. Sprinkle with bread crumbs and dot with butter. Bake 25 minutes at 350°. Serves 6-8.

VELDA'S CRISP CARROT CASSEROLE

8 large carrots or 20 ounces
   frozen carrots
¼ cup chopped onion

⅓ cup sugar
½ cup chopped celery
½ cup mayonnaise

Put carrots in saucepan with the onion and sugar in enough water just to cover. Cook until carrots are tender. Pour off water, add salt and pepper to taste. Add remaining ingredients. Place in buttered casserole and bake at 350° for 30 minutes.

MIZ FRANKIE'S APRICOT CASSEROLE

3 large cans apricots, drained
   and mashed
1½ tubes of Ritz cracker
   (crushed)

1 cup brown sugar
1 stick melted butter

In round casserole, place half of mashed apricots, layer ½ of cracker crumbs and ½ of brown sugar. Repeat layers. Pour melted butter over all. Bake at 350° for 20-25 minutes until bubbly. Serves 6-8.

VELDA'S PEAR SALAD

1 cup raw grated carrots
juice and grated rind of 1 lemon
½ cup sugar

canned pear halves
lettuce leaves

Combine first 3 ingredients. Let stand overnight. Drain well. Fill pear halves and serve on lettuce.

RUBY D'S CAKE

1 can cherry pie filling
1 can (No. 2½) crushed
   pineapple (with juice)
1 box yellow cake mix

2 sticks margarine (melted)
1 can coconut
1 cup chopped pecans

In bottom of pyrex dish place pie filling and pineapple. Sprinkle with cake mix. Pour melted margarine over cake mix. Top with coconut and pecans. Bake at 350° for approximately 1 hour.

VELDA'S SWEDISH PIE

½ cup cake flour (regular flour
   minus 1 tablespoon)
2 teaspoons baking powder
½ teaspoon salt
2 eggs

1 cup firmly packed light brown
   sugar
1 teaspoon vanilla
1 cup chopped pecans
1 cup tart apples, peeled and
   cubed

Combine flour, baking powder and salt; set aside.

Beat eggs and sugar until light and fluffy. Add flour mixture to egg mixture, blending well. Stir in vanilla, pecans and apples. Spread mixture in greased 10-inch pie plate. Bake at 350° for 30 minutes. Cool, cut into wedges and serve with whipped cream or other dairy topping.

BROCCOLI SALAD

1 cup mayonnaise
½ cup sugar
¼ cup chopped onion
2 tablespoons vinegar

2 bunches broccoli
1 cup raisins
bacon bits

Mix mayonnaise, sugar, onion, and vinegar. Toss with broccoli florets and raisins. Sprinkle bacon bits on top.

CRANBERRY CASSEROLE

2 cups unpeeled raw apples, chopped
2 cups raw cranberries
1¼ cups white sugar
½ cup brown sugar

⅓ cup pecans, chopped
½ cup melted margarine
1½ cups quick oats (dry)
⅓ cup flour
dash of cinnamon

In 2 quart dish, combine apples, cranberries and white sugar. Top with mixture of remaining ingredients. Bake at 350° for 60 minutes or until lightly browned. Serve hot with chicken or turkey.

E.J.'S EASY CHICKEN TETRAZZINI

2 cups cooked white meat chicken
1 medium onion
2 tablespoons butter
¼ cup finely chopped bell pepper
2 cans cream of chicken soup (undiluted)

2 cans cream of celery soup (undiluted)
1 small jar chopped pimento
1 small jar sliced cooked mushrooms (drained)
pinch pepper
1 cup cooking sherry
1 box vermicelli spaghetti

Saute chopped onion in butter. Add peppers. Stir in chicken and celery soups and add chicken. Add pimento and mushrooms. Sprinkle in pepper and pour in cooking sherry. Cook slowly for about 20 minutes. Cook spaghetti according to directions and drain. Stir in chicken mixture. Serves 6.

COCONUT CARAMEL PIE

¼ cup butter
1 7-ounce package coconut
½ cup chopped pecans
1 8-ounce package cream
    cheese
1 14-ounce can sweetened
    condensed milk

1 16-ounce package prepared
    whipped topping
1 12-ounce jar caramel ice
    cream topping
2 deep dish pie shells

Melt butter in a large skillet. Add coconut and pecans; cook until golden brown, stirring frequently. Set mixture aside. Combine cream cheese and condensed milk; beat until smooth. Fold in whipped topping. Layer ¼ cream cheese mixture in each pie shell. Drizzle ¼ caramel topping over each. Sprinkle ¼ coconut mixture on each. Repeat layers with remaining ingredients. Cover and freeze until firm. Let pie stand at room temperature 5 minutes before slicing. Makes 2 pies.

ROTTEN COCONUT CAKE

1 box white cake mix
1 can cream of coconut
1 can sweetened condensed
    milk

1 small can coconut
1 medium package prepared
    whipped topping

Bake cake as directed on box in 9x13-inch pan. When cake is done, punch holes in cake with fork. Mix cream of coconut and condensed milk together and pour over hot cake. Let cool. Top with whipped topping and coconut.

MAMA'S CHRISTMAS FUDGE

3 cups semi-sweet chocolate
    chips
3 small almond Hershey bars
2 cups marshmallow cream
¼ cup butter

4 cups chopped nuts (at least
    half almonds)
1⅔ cups undiluted evaporated
    milk
4½ cups sugar

Put chocolate chips, Hershey bars, marshmallow cream, butter and nuts in large mixing bowl. Combine milk and sugar in saucepan, boil for 5 minutes or 225° on candy thermometer. Stir mixture constantly to keep from sticking. Remove from heat and pour over ingredients in mixing bowl. Stir with wooden spoon until chocolate is smooth. Spread on greased surface and cut in squares when cool. Yield: 4-5 dozen squares. (From **Woman's Exchange Cook Book**).

INDEX

Mail to:

**Hemlock Inn
Bryson City, N.C. 28713**

Please send me _____ copies of Recipes from Our Front Porch at
$12.95 per copy. I am including $3.00 to cover postage and handling.
(North Carolina residents add .78 sales tax per book.) Enclosed is my
check or money order for $ _____ .

Name _____

Address_____

City _____ State _____ Zip _____

Mail to:

**Hemlock Inn
Bryson City, N.C. 28713**

Please send me _____ copies of Recipes from Our Front Porch at
$12.95 per copy. I am including $3.00 to cover postage and handling.
(North Carolina residents add .78 sales tax per book.) Enclosed is my
check or money order for $ _____ .

Name _____

Address_____

City _____ State _____ Zip _____

Mail to:

**Hemlock Inn
Bryson City, N.C. 28713**

Please send me _____ copies of Recipes from Our Front Porch at
$12.95 per copy. I am including $3.00 to cover postage and handling.
(North Carolina residents add .78 sales tax per book.) Enclosed is my
check or money order for $ _____ .

Name _____

Address_____

City _____ State _____ Zip _____

Re-Order Additional Copies